BIRDS
IN YOUR GARDEN

BIRDS
IN YOUR GARDEN

How to attract and identify over 70 common species

Nigel Wood

PEERAGE BOOKS

ACKNOWLEDGEMENTS

PHOTOGRAPHS

Aquila Photographics: 30 (T); W.S. Paton 69 (T); J.L. Roberts 57 (B); M.C. Wilkes 89 (T).
Ardea: J.A. Bailey 52 (B), 131 (T), 150 (B); J.B. and S. Bottomley 29 (T); W. Curth 89 (BR).
Frank V. Blackburn 71 (T), 90–1, 110 (T), 111 (T), 149 (T). R.J.C. Blewitt 71 (B). Arne
Blomgren 149 (C). Arthur Christiansen 111 (B). Bruce Coleman Ltd: Jane Burton 12 (B);
Stephen Dalton 129 (T); E. Duscher 131 (CB); Udo Hirsch 70 (B); Gordon Langsbury 70 (T);
John Markham 72 (TL); D. Middleton 112 (T); S.C. Porter 72 (TR), 109 (T). Format
Publishing Services: Derek Hall 152 (T). Francisco Futil 49. Roy A. Harris and K.R. Duff 90
(T). David Hosking 152 (B). Eric Hosking 30 (B), 129 (B). Jacana: Brosselin 31; Ducrot 131
(CT); F. Henrion 130 (BL); Claude Nardin 151 (C); Robert 151 (B); R. Volot 150 (T); Albert
Visage 91 (B). E.A. Janes 72 (C). Frank Lane: Heinz Schrempp 132 (B); Eichorn/Zingel 69
(B). François Merlet 52 (TR). Mike Mockler 9, 12 (T). Natural History Photographic
Agency: Frank V. Blackburn 92 (B); D.N. Dalton 132 (T); Stephen Dalton 51, 89 (B), 109
(C), 130 (T); Walter J.C. Murray 52 (TL), 110 (B). Natural Science Photos: C.A. Walker 29
(C). Nature Photographers Ltd: Paul Sterry 32 (B). Photo Researchers Inc: 92 (T). R.
Roberts 112 (B). Ilkka Virkkunen 90 (B). Wildlife Studies Ltd: 32 (T), 72 (B), 112 (C), 130
(C), 131 (B), 132 (TL).

While every effort has been made to obtain permission for the publication of all copyright
material it is possible that we may inadvertently have failed to obtain the necessary
permission. In all cases we offer our apologies to the copyright owners.

ILLUSTRATIONS

Colour illustrations by Noel Cusa, Robert Morton/Linden Artists, John Rignall and Ian
Willis

Line drawings by Brin Edwards/Format Publishing Services, Ian Garrard, Robert Gillmor,
Leslie Greenwood, Ron Hayward, Robert Morton and Phil Weare/Linden Artists and Meg
Rutherford

Edited and designed by Format Publishing Services, 10A The Parade, Chandler's Ford,
Eastleigh, Hants, England

First published in Great Britain in 1985 by
Hamlyn Publishing

This edition published in 1989 by
Peerage Books
Michelin House, 81 Fulham Road, London SW3 6RB

Copyright © Hamlyn Publishing 1985
a division of The Hamlyn Publishing Group Ltd.

ISBN 1 85052 134 4

Printed in Spain

Lito. A. Romero, S. A. – D. L. TF. 23-1989

Contents

Introduction

Birds are our most noticeable form of wildlife, and for many people the most attractive, too. Many species go about their lives in full view of our windows: feeding, drinking, bathing, preening, courting, mating, building nests and raising their young for all our enjoyment if we care to watch. With their powers of flight, birds are not constrained by man-made barriers and, just like a seed finding a fertile piece of ground, birds will find the sympathetic plot of land that has been prepared with them in mind. It is the aim of this book to show that, with thought, any garden may be enhanced to attract wildlife, particularly birds.

First will come the opportunists: the house sparrows and starlings, attracted by the food you have put out. Their noisy antics are all some town-dwellers know of bird life but, with a little space, a small financial outlay and some patience, your garden can become much more than just a backyard where a few birds occasionally come to feed. If you have a lawn, blackbirds and song thrushes will arrive and, as your planting begins to take shape, dunnocks and wrens, and the confiding robin will also visit your garden to feed. The addition of a nest box may give you the pleasure of watching a pair of blue tits raise a family of eight or ten youngsters.

You will wake to a serenade of bird song, finding that with familiarity you are able to recognize the different species by their songs. Many garden birds like to sing from an exposed perch, so you will have a good view of them as they advertize for mates and let their rivals know that they have established territory. Not all birds sing, but most have recognizable calls. One such is the blue tit, which is probably our most numerous nest box user. By providing nest sites, artificial or natural, you can help the birds at this crucial time, and enjoy following the fortunes of your nesting birds.

Some birds are seasonal, and these include swallows and house martins which come here to raise their families in summer but leave when insect food becomes scarce. Providing food in winter may attract birds that usually breed away from the garden, like coal tits. Sometimes these birds are joined by winter visitors such as redwings and fieldfares from Scandinavia and, exceptionally, the exotic waxwing, which almost invariably visits gardens in its search for berries.

With shelter for nesting and roosting, plentiful food in the form of berries and insects, and water to drink and bathe in, your garden will become a haven for birds. But creating the best kind of garden for birds brings other rewards, too. Just as woodland birds found our cultivation suitable to their way of life so many centuries ago, so other animals and plants will find your garden a safer place to live than the countryside beyond the town. Plant seeds flourish in soil that is enriched with natural composts and where herbicides are unknown. Frogs and toads come to unpolluted garden ponds to spawn. Insects seek nectar and food-plants for their larvae, and without the threat of premature death from insecticide sprays, pollinate the flowers and provide abundant food for hungry nestlings. Into your small sanctuary waddles a hedgehog, making his home in your compost heap and spending his nights gobbling up the slugs that had intended to eat your young lettuces.

These and the other creatures in your garden will form an ecological unit, with each creature playing its part in the overall balance of things. Sometimes you will find that your garden guests will 'bite the hand that feeds them', a swarm of caterpillars defoliating a shrub or bullfinches descending on your fruit buds, and you may have to intervene. But you will have noticed that a few days after aphids have appeared on your roses so have the ladybirds that feed on them, and just when you despaired of the snails eating all your tender young leaves, your resident song thrush works its way methodically through them, clearing one patch of the garden after another. So in a natural community there is a balance of sorts, self regulating without the intervention of man and his harmful chemicals.

In your own way you will have become part of a movement that is not only bringing wildlife back into towns, but also providing a refuge for our hard-pressed animals and plants. For many hundreds of years our wildlife found a home in the countryside that we created, because the pace of change was gradual and there was time to adapt. A remarkable diversity of habitat evolved which favoured most wildlife except those creatures that came into direct competition with us. Recently the pace of change has become so rapid, and the style of agriculture and forestry so uniform, that large parts of the countryside are becoming inhospitable to all but the most adaptable of our wild animals and plants.

As individuals we *can* do something to redress the balance, by bringing a little piece of the natural world into our own back gardens and creating a natural haven for birds and other creatures in which to flourish.

Planning and planting

So the exercise seems worthwhile. How then to start? Just as the ideal bird garden will be an excellent habitat for other wildlife, it is worth stressing that your bird garden should also be one of beauty and year-round interest for you. With the recent upsurge of interest in gardening for wildlife there has been perhaps too much emphasis placed on the 'wild patch', with its nettles and other weeds, dead timber and compost heaps. While all these things may be part of the ideal space for birds, one of the aims of this book is to show that a garden that is both attractive and fulfils all the usual recreational needs can also be a wildlife habitat. There are very few of us who have time to ensure a totally weed-free garden, so the 'ones that get away' plus a few deliberately cultivated 'weeds', for example thistles and teasels, may well suffice.

What will be true of the garden based on this book is that it will contain mainly native species of plants, will have few (though some) of the showier flowers, and will have an emphasis on the shrubbery and perennial herbaceous border rather than on annual flower beds and bedding plants. What it will also have is an absolute minimum of insecticides and chemical fertilizers, so if you are an advocate of weedkillers and phosphates some parts of this book may make uncomfortable reading!

Finally, your garden is first and foremost just that – yours. If you wish only to cut the grass occasionally and otherwise never set foot in the place, content instead to watch the wildlife undisturbed from your window, then that is your choice. But most of us will want to sit in the garden at least, and for many the activity of gardening itself is a most pleasurable and relaxing experience. So my advice is to use your garden as much as you like, being mindful of the needs of those creatures you have intentionally attracted.

The first essentials in all types of gardening are the same: consideration of the soil type and garden aspect, and planning on paper. As this book is primarily about birds I do not propose to go into the detail of pH types and soil tests here. That information can be found readily in any gardening book. What I will say on the subject is this: that for every soil type there is a natural flora. There are very few areas of Britain that will not support woodland, when free from the threat of grazing or fire. Find out what plants are contained in woodland in your area and approximate these as near as possible. They will certainly attract the usual garden birds, and depending on your situation some local specialities, too. In the wildlife garden we are trying to create something of a woodland edge habitat, but of course our woodland birds have also learned to live in farmland hedgerows for centuries. Another piece of advice is 'don't try to

Opposite: A 'wild' garden. Apart from the bird table, the hanging feeder and nest box on the rowan, and the water for drinking and bathing, other features include the tree stump left to rot, the brambles (excellent cover for small birds) and the patch of nettles that will feed butterfly caterpillars. The mature beech in the background will have its own attractions to birds, as will the hedge and rhododendron.

_____t: Cover for nesting ___s, fragrant with ____ctar which can attract ___me spectacular moths, ___and bearing berries that tits and warblers will eat, make honeysuckle a must for the wildlife garden.

Right: _The barberry's flowers, which attract insects, are followed by a stunning display of berries upon which blackbirds and thrushes will feast._

Right: _Michaelmas daisies create a splash of colour in the flower border in late autumn. They also provide nectar for late-flying small tortoiseshell butterflies._

Right: *Cover for nesting birds, fragrant with nectar which can attract some spectacular moths, and bearing berries that tits and warblers will eat, make honeysuckle a must for the wildlife garden.*

Right: *The barberry's flowers, which attract insects, are followed by a stunning display of berries upon which blackbirds and thrushes will feast.*

Right: *Michaelmas daisies create a splash of colour in the flower border in late autumn. They also provide nectar for late-flying small tortoiseshell butterflies.*

Above: *If you don't harvest the fruit yourself for crab-apple jelly, the various members of the thrush family will appreciate your gift!*

Left: *Wall cover blends a house with its surroundings and softens the hard outlines of a building. Providing it is adequately supported, a wall climber will not damage your property. Virginia creeper, shown here, is a favoured nest site of the spotted flycatcher.*

Above: *A male pied
flycatcher returns to the
nest box with food for
the young. Like many
woodland birds that will
nest in gardens,
flycatchers feed huge
quantities of defoliating
caterpillars to their
broods. Note the metal
plate around the
entrance hole to prevent
predators widening the
access to gain entry.*

Right: *Tits are our most
acrobatic garden feeders,
and will cling readily to
devices that leave the less
adept sparrows and
starlings with no chance
of obtaining a foothold.
This hanging feeder
would be ideal for
dispensing bird pudding.
Here a great tit and a
coal tit are feeding side
by side, with a blue tit in
the background.*

fight the geology'. If your garden is in the middle of a moorland peat bog, there will be little point in altering the soil so that you can plant to attract bullfinches, unless you have a very substantial plot! On the other hand you may be able to provide some cover that will act as a beacon to the tired migrant. But your staple fare will be moorland birds. In the suburbs, however, an established garden is likely to have had its basic soil improved, as will those of the neighbours. See what grows well in their gardens and you will have a shrewd idea of what should grow well in yours, assuming a similar aspect. If you do take over an existing garden, be patient and live with it for a year before undertaking anything too radical. That unsightly clump of twigs may turn into an attractive bush in summer, and the boring conifer you intended grubbing out, reveals itself in winter as a vital roost for finches.

If your house is new then you can create your ideal, once you've removed the builder's rubble. If your soil is at one of the extremes, being composed of either clay or sand, it may be worth improving it before you

No garden plan can be regarded as definitive, since so much depends on the size and shape of your plot. Most of the features shown below can be incorporated in the smaller garden, but you may have to restrict yourself to fewer shrubs and trees, and content yourself with a drinking pool instead of a pond.

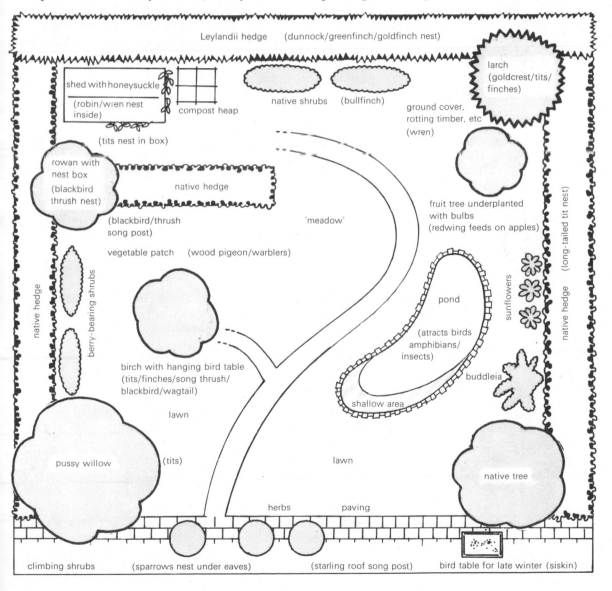

go any further. On clay soil, improving the drainage can be effected by siting a pond that fills naturally away from the house. On both soil types avoid digging deep, for this will bring up subsoil and stones, and add plenty of manure. Plan your garden on graph paper, marking existing features you wish to retain. Then draw your changes on tracing paper which you use as an overlay. This gives you the freedom to change your mind as you work things out, without having to rub out half your garden every time you have a new idea. Take into consideration the aspect of the garden and the sight lines from the house, and allow for at least two positions for a bird table. Hard surfaces are essential for you to walk on if you intend replenishing a bird table throughout the winter, so this needs to be thought about at an early stage, too. Although meandering paths are attractive, the logical route is invariably the most direct. Route paths directly if the access is clear, especially if children use the garden regularly. If you don't want straight paths, then plant obstacles to route your path round, or you will rue the day.

Your aim is to provide birds with food, water, shelter and sites for nesting and feeding. This will necessitate a range of plant species, from grass to trees. As trees are the most dominant element it is best to consider these first.

TREES

Birds use trees principally as lookout posts and as a refuge from danger. They may use them as song posts and, if suitable, will also nest in them. They also find food in most native and some exotic species – either in the form of the insects that dwell on the plant or the fruits that the tree produces. Our 'top ten' deciduous trees for invertebrate life are, in descending order of value: oak, willow, birch, hawthorn, poplar, alder, crab apple, elm, hazel, beech. To these can be added two useful conifers, Scots pine and larch – which are also listed in order of value. Some of these are unsuitable for all except the largest gardens, but of the deciduous trees, birch is both fast growing and casts only a light shade, and will tolerate most soils. In addition to its value for invertebrates, its seeds attract siskins and redpolls to feed. Hawthorn will make a standard tree, but has added value as a hedging plant, and is discussed later. The same applies to the hazel. Poplars are to be avoided in all but the largest gardens as they are thirsty and put out extensive root systems. On clay soils in a dry year they can extract the last drop of moisture from the soil and cause the clay to shrink and crack so that subsidence occurs. Alder and crab apple both provide a home for a wide range of insects, and bear fruit that will attract birds – in the case of alder, redpolls and siskins, and in the case of crab apple, members of the thrush family. If the fruits stay on the tree long enough they may be taken by redwings and fieldfares in winter when shortages bring them into the garden in search of food.

It would be nice to be able to recommend the planting of elm, but until a Dutch elm disease-resistant strain is found the exercise seems futile. This is sad, since the elm not only provides a home for about eighty species of invertebrates, but in later years is also a great provider of nest sites in the form of holes. Like the oak and willow, elms are really on a different size scale to the previously mentioned tree species. If you have

After the inevitable pruning, try rooting the cuttings. They are an ideal way of helping to increase plant cover inexpensively.

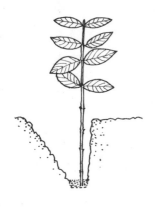

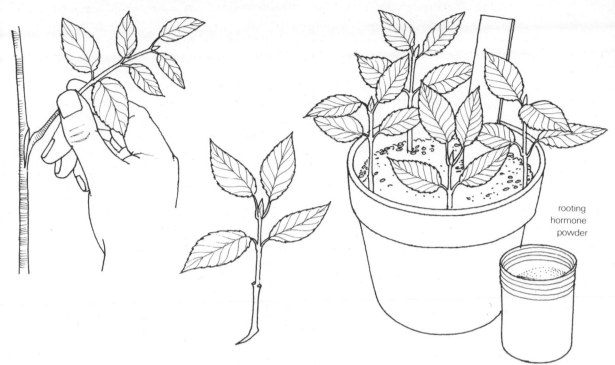

Propagation from cuttings. First, take a cutting to include a heel; next, insert into rooting powder, and place cuttings around edge of pot filled with compost. Water in, and cover cuttings with a polythene bag to prevent the soil drying out.

rooting
hormone
powder

elm stumps on your boundary, however, interplant with some other species as standards and allow the elm to regenerate as scrub. This will form an effective barrier and will not be overlooked by nesting birds, including such relative garden rarities as lesser whitethroat and turtle dove in southern England, the elm's former stronghold. If the disease reappears (as is almost invariably the case), cut the hedge to its base and let the process repeat itself. You will simply be managing your elm as coppice, a traditional practice much respected by conservationists for the value of natural cyclical regeneration it encourages. If you live in the Midlands, your elm scrub could help to keep the scarce white-letter hairstreak going through times which are bleak for a butterfly which lays its eggs on this endangered tree.

Beech, when mature, is also rather large for most gardens, but if you have space and time you will find it a most attractive tree throughout the seasons. It supports about sixty species of invertebrates and its fruit, the beech mast, is a favourite of bramblings, hawfinches, chaffinches and jays.

For those who may be in a position to influence planting in the larger-than-average garden, or even in the countryside or in a public space, then the value of a mature oak or willow cannot be over-emphasized. Oak is practically a habitat in itself; it supports about 300 varieties of invertebrates, it has the ability to provide a home for many birds and even mammals, and its rich crop of acorns are beloved of jays. Willows have about fifty species less to boast, but that is still a formidable number. My neighbour's weeping willow (which practically touches their house in their fairly small garden) is rarely without avian inhabitants, and is the main source of visitors to my own garden, which I am still in the process of converting to a bird garden from its former use as a market garden. I'm so impressed I've planted one myself, and trust that it will look so good that future owners will leave it unmolested. Of course as it develops it will shade out some other plants, but I am fortunate in having enough space still to provide a variety of planting for the birds.

For the bird gardener who really wants these species but has little space then there is a solution. Plant a few acorns in a hedge and let them come up with the other hedging. You then treat them like the rest of the hedge – as you can see in roadside hedges throughout the south-east. They will not have acorns, but their value to insect life will remain. If you want a willow, substitute a pussy willow for the larger specimens. This attracts a host of insects, and is invaluable in that it flowers long before most other trees (witch-hazel being an exception) bringing the early bird to feed. Pussy willows do not grow very large, and have quite a pleasing shape. If you want to keep one very small, treat it like a shrub. (See the pruning illustration on page 35.) In fact this is the solution to any size problems. After all, the beech in the hedge that keeps its leaves throughout the winter is the same type as the ninety-foot specimens growing in the Chilterns, the only difference is in their management.

Three more deciduous trees need to be named. Rowan, and its close relative whitebeam, are both fairly fast growing, upright in habit, bear attractive white flowers in early summer and berries that birds like in early autumn. They also make excellent song posts and reasonable nest sites. Finally, apple, or for that matter most orchard trees, are suitable for the bird garden provided you can be philosophical about fruit losses due to birds. Apples in particular develop natural holes in old age and the stored windfalls of these and pears are a favourite of fieldfares, redwings, thrushes and blackbirds when snow covers the ground.

Scots pine is our most important native conifer, and supports its own biotope (the collection of dependent plants and animals) in Scotland in the remnants of the old Caledonian Forest. In the garden it will provide shelter all year round, attract its own dependent insects, and is the tree

Layering is ideal for low-growing shrubs – some of which 'layer' naturally. Choose a lax branch (A) and make an upward slit in the stem. Peg the cut portion of the stem down and cover with soil (B). The layered portion can be detached when it has rooted. In air layering (C) a cut is made in the stem and the slit is held open and surrounded with sphagnum moss and polythene. The stem is removed when it has rooted.

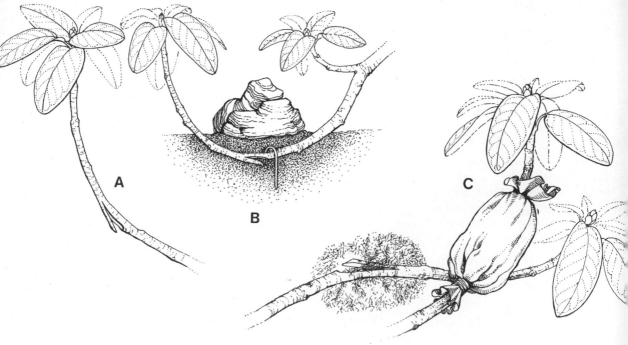

most likely to entice wandering crossbills into the garden. In the forest situation the lower branches tend to die off as the tree matures, but in a garden you may have to remove these branches to prevent too dense a shade from forming. Larch is a most attractive tree in its fresh green spring foliage, but although it is a conifer it is not evergreen. It grows quickly and produces valuable seed that brings finches, and sometimes their close allies, crossbills, to feed. About twenty types of invertebrate are also found on larches. For cover alone, or to provide a song post in a small tree-less garden, the hedging cypresses – Leyland or Lawson's – will grow quickly and occupy only a small area when planted singly. Their rather regular shape can be broken up by planting them with some other shrubs and ground cover. In their first years they may need protection from frost and cold, drying winds.

GROWING AND PLANTING YOUNG TREES

Growing trees from seed is fairly easy, and is recommended as a cheap source of trees for a garden which already has some tree cover. Many gardening experts advise stratification and other methods to encourage propagation, and of course they do work, but so does nature. I harvest the seed when its ready – still on the tree but ripe – cover with a minimum of soil, keep the area weed free, and allow two years if necessary to germinate. My success rate is not bad. (I avoid pots, because the soil dries out rapidly, unless the pot itself is buried.) Another neglected method for propagating trees is by cuttings, and is particularly effective (and cheap) with willows and poplars in early spring. Take a semi-ripe shoot about 50 cm (18 in) long, strip off all but the top two or three leaves, dip in a rooting compound and insert in the ground for two-thirds of its length. Water thoroughly and cover with a plastic bottle sawn in half if there are drying winds or unseasonal sunshine. This technique is also successful with a great variety of native shrubs, which can be culled from friends' and neighbours' hedges (with their permission) and used to establish your own mixed hedge.

If you have no trees in the garden, then you will probably want to plant saplings. Garden centres stock most native trees, but it is often worth checking in local directories for nurseries who will supply less popular varieties as well as the common ones for about half the price of a garden centre. The drawback is that these trees will be bare-rooted and can only be planted when dormant, from November to March. Evergreens transplant best in early spring. Choose a site that will give your tree the space it needs to grow to maturity. Most trees in gardens are planted on boundaries, but do avoid planting near walls where the soil dries out and the tree grows distorted. Remember, too, that your neighbour may not appreciate your planting and lop any branches that come over his land, which could produce lots of shrubby growth on that side and will certainly make for an odd-shaped tree. Refer to gardening books for advice on mulching, pruning and protection against frost.

Planting can be done in all weathers except after a hard frost or when the soil is waterlogged, but will be easiest and most pleasant on a mild, windless day. Excavate a hole that will easily take the whole root-ball, placing the excavated soil on to a polythene sheet or similar. This soil will take up about three times as much space as the hole it has come from! If you're planting in grass, remove enough turfs to make the job easy, but leave one out when replacing to give a bare area around the base of the tree. This means the tree receives more rain and nourishment, and in dry weather a bucketful of water can be carefully poured round your tree without eroding the soil.

Having reached the correct depth (check the already present soil mark on the stem of your sapling), loosen the soil down to another 15 cm (6 in), add a little compost (not artificial fertilizer or manure), and settle the tree into the hole. If you're working single-handed, a plank placed across the hole on either side of the tree will keep it in place and upright while you position your supporting stake, pushing it into the loosened soil at the base of the hole, and taking care not to upset the roots. You can then carefully shovel your soil back in, working the earth all around the roots with your hands to ensure there are no air pockets. Once the roots are well covered you can firm the soil with your foot, but don't stamp. Packed soil will not allow in water and air. Water generously, but don't allow the soil to become waterlogged.

Careful planting and correct staking ensure the best possible prospects for a sapling.

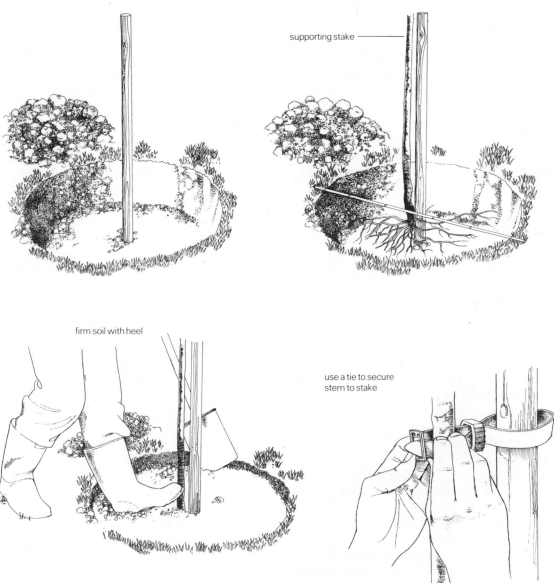

supporting stake

firm soil with heel

use a tie to secure stem to stake

HEDGING

Whatever the size of your garden, it will have at least two boundaries. Depending on the aspect of your garden, you should be able to hedge along one side at least, giving protection against domestic cats, and natural predators, too, and sheltering your plants. From the wildlife point of view it enables you to recreate the potential for nest sites, shelter, and the opportunities for insects and the natural harvest that our native shrubs provide, in the minimum of space. In a larger garden a hedge may be introduced across the garden to separate the recreational from the vegetable plot, or to screen a shed or compost heap. As previously mentioned, most native trees can be hedged, but generally they will not bear fruit when cut back regularly. Depending on its ultimate size, it may be possible to trim the hedge once every two years in order to encourage production of fruit. Of the species mentioned earlier, hawthorn and hazel make an ideal basis for a mixed hedge. Hawthorn is an excellent defence against mammalian intruders and is probably the favourite nest site for hedgerow birds. It should be laid in its early years to make the base of the hedge mammal-proof. A less refined method of achieving the same result is to cut the young trunks back after two years to about 5 cm (2 in) above the ground, which has the effect of producing a mass of new shoots from that point the following spring. In May your hawthorn will be covered in fragrant white blooms, a source of nectar for insects, and in autumn the birds will come for the berries. Hazel, too, will produce fruit if not too ruthlessly trimmed – the nuts being a favourite of nuthatches, coal tits, squirrels and dormice – and insects will come to the catkins that appear in spring.

Other native shrubs suitable for the mixed hedge are blackthorn, wild privet (which has thorns and bears black berries, a favourite of bullfinches), and the guelder rose, which is really a viburnum. To give this entirely deciduous hedge a green look in winter you could plant the evergreen variety of honeysuckle, which also bears fruit that titmice and warblers like. For a truly wild look, you can also add bramble and wild roses, and none of this need cost you a penny! All these can be grown from seed, from cuttings, or from creeping stems that are rooting. If you have problems getting wild stock, then hawthorn (or quickthorn, as horti-culturalists may call it) for hedging can be bought cheaply at most garden centres. The young plants will be no more than 45 cm (18 in) long, will probably be bundled, and are known as whips. If I wanted to plant a dozen or so hawthorn trees I would certainly start with these, because once established they soon catch up with their more advanced brethren. For hedging, plant 30 cm (12 in) apart, interspersing with other plants as you like. It's best to hoe between the young plants for the first two years to give them the best chance, but after that why not let other plants colonize naturally, or even introduce garden-grown varieties of typical hedgerow flowers like violets, primroses, bluebells and the campions (it is illegal to dig up wild specimens although you may collect seed). If in doubt, consult your nearest roadside hedge!

The bridge between the 'wild' hedge and traditional evergreen hedges are those of beech and hornbeam. As mentioned previously, when hedged these species hold their leaves through winter until the new leaves appear. Beech and copper beech are usually obtainable from nurseries as hedging

When making a hedge it is much easier to plant your 'whips' into a trench than to dig lots of individual holes for each plant.

whips, like hawthorn. For hornbeam, you may have to hunt around a bit, but if you are gardening on clay it may be worth the effort. Hawthorn is also quite happy on clay, but beeches will thrive on chalk, as will yew, box and holly. None of these is likely to fruit as hedges, however, so their value is mainly as year-round cover, suitable for roosting and nesting alike. The drawback of yew is that the berries (or kernels) are poisonous, as are the cuttings if eaten by livestock. The pinky-orange berries of the spindle, a native deciduous shrub, are also poisonous, and both are to be avoided if children and livestock may be put at risk. For a fast-growing evergreen hedge, the cypress varieties Leyland and Lawson's cannot be beaten. They will screen your garden very efficiently and make excellent cover. Dunnocks, goldfinches and greenfinches may nest in these hedges and, if the tops are left untrimmed and the plant produces seed, siskins and redpolls will feed on them. Unlike the native deciduous hedge, however, you will not be able to underplant as the ground beneath the hedge will be in deep shade and tends to be dry.

Whatever the composition of your hedge, trim it with care so that nesting birds are not disturbed and developing fruit is not removed – two good arguments for trimming in early spring. The hedge should be trimmed into an 'A' shape so that the lower foliage receives light and air, ensuring that this part of the hedge, so vital in keeping out the enemies of birds, is healthy.

If you live on the coast then your hedge will be of double value, protecting your garden plants from wind-borne salt and providing shelter for tired migrants. An outer defence of trees could be planted of which sycamore and clustered pine are suitable. Among or behind this blackthorn, gorse, spindle and tamarisk will all cope with the wind and the salt. Supreme among the salt-tolerant shrubs though is sea buckthorn, which is found at a number of bird observatories where its cover is host to thousands of migrants. In autumn our summer migrants feed in its cover while stocking up for their southward journey, mingling with tired immigrants such as redwings and fieldfares, which feast on the bright orange berries.

SHRUBS

Behind the outer defence of the hedge, shrubs can provide food in the form of berries, cover for roosting and nesting, and give your garden year-round colour. Of the cultivated varieties cotoneasters and barberries (*Berberis*) are excellent, but the humble elder is probably the best of all. It comes into leaf early – in milder parts some leaves stay on the bush through the winter until the gales of March, by which time the new leaves are forming – is attractive in flower and fruits generously. It attracts blackbirds, thrushes, blackcaps, willow warblers, wood pigeons – in fact most birds that will eat berries including a number of insect-eating summer migrants that turn to fruit in order to build up their reserves of fat before the long journey south. Among its other virtues are that it is tolerant of poor soil and ruthless pruning. I have three in my garden – one for the flowers to make elderflower champagne, one for the berries (for elderberry pie) and one for the birds.

Of the cotoneasters, only one is to be avoided, *Conspicuax decora*, because birds ignore the berries. Recommended are *Cotoneaster cornubia*, strong growing and bearing the largest berries, *C.bullatus*, evergreen and fruiting over an extended period, and *C.horizontalis*, clothing walls with its dark green herringbone foliage and making good ground cover.

Equally versatile are the barberries. *Berberis thunbergii* is good for hedging and disliked by dogs, *B.darwinii* is evergreen with attractive flowers and purple fruit, and *B.wilsonae* is deciduous and a heavy fruiter. A browse round a garden centre looking at barberries and cotoneasters is advised. Other cultivated and decorative shrubs are *Skimmia japonica*, whose insect-attracting flowers are followed by bright red berries which remain throughout the winter, *Callicarpa*, which has beautiful autumn tints before the purple berries are revealed, and *Pernettya*, whose berries may be white, pink, red or purple. These three all need to have both male and female plants close to each other to ensure that the flowers are cross-pollinated to form fruit. *Viburnum*, of which there are spring and summer flowering varieties, have already been mentioned, and snowberry is another useful shrub.

Some native shrubs which birds (and insects) will appreciate are alder and purging buckthorn, dogwood (*Cornus*), which is usually grown for the colour of its stems but also flowers and produces berries, and sallow, whose early catkins attract the first insects in spring followed by chiffchaffs and willow warblers which need their insect food, however early in the year it is.

Other shrubs which birds visit for their insects are *Hebe* (which is evergreen and has white, pink, purple or blue flowers), lavender, and *Arbutus*, the strawberry tree, which flowers and fruits at the same time in late autumn, on sunny days attracting butterflies like red admirals, peacocks and small tortoiseshells. The butterfly bush par excellence is

Buddleia, whose fragrant blooms on arching stems can be host to dozens of butterflies at a time. Purple and white varieties are available, although the butterflies seem to prefer the purple type. Another shrub beloved of insects is the bramble. Sometimes the fruit is eagerly devoured by birds – bullfinches eating the seeds in the berries when it is old – but the real value of bramble for birds is the way it grows over obstacles, creating excellent nesting cover for wrens and warblers. Soft fruits like redcurrants, raspberries and blackcurrants could also be grown for the benefit of the birds, although it will be a strong-willed bird lover who leaves the strawberries for them!

An attractive shrub that can be part of a hedge, free-standing, or trained against a wall is *Pyracantha*, the firethorn. Evergreen, with masses of white blossom in June, it produces clusters of scarlet berries in autumn. Its thorns make it a good nest site, and when wall trained and pruned the knotty spurs that result make even better positions for nests. Honeysuckle, which once established can be pruned like a hedge, also makes a good nest site. It has a gorgeous scent evocative of a summer's evening, is visited by moths, and after flowering bears berries that the birds will take. A wall-trained *Japonica* will feed thrushes in late winter if the quince-like fruits are left, and the attractive climbing *Hydrangea* will clothe a wall and conceal nests. Wall climbers are the best way of providing a natural nest site for spotted flycatchers, so Russian vine, *Clematis*, *Wisteria*, which all have attractive flowers and a long flowering period, are also worth planting. And of course an open-fronted nest box is more likely to be occupied if there is cover around. Virginia creeper and ivy, two self clingers, are excellent for cladding a house. The flowers of ivy are host to many insects late in the year, and the leaves are a protection in winter to dormant larvae. The berries come in early spring when other supplies may be exhausted, and are widely exploited by thrushes, blackbirds and wood pigeons.

Keeping the ground weed free under your developing shrubs can be a chore, but if you plant ground-covering shrubs you can cut out the weeding and help wildlife at the same time. Wrens, dunnocks and any warblers that may come into the garden tend to keep in low cover or feed

Although an introduced species, Buddleia *is second to none for attracting butterflies.* Cotoneaster horizontalis *is decorative, with red berries and foliage in autumn, and provides cover and food for birds.*

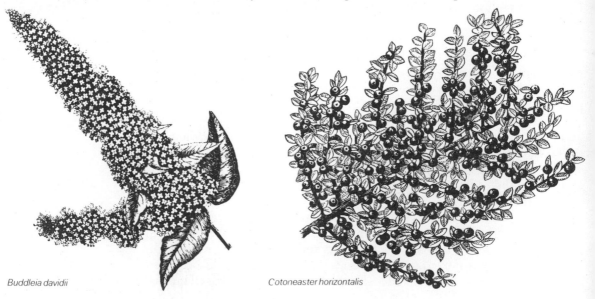

Buddleia davidii

Cotoneaster horizontalis

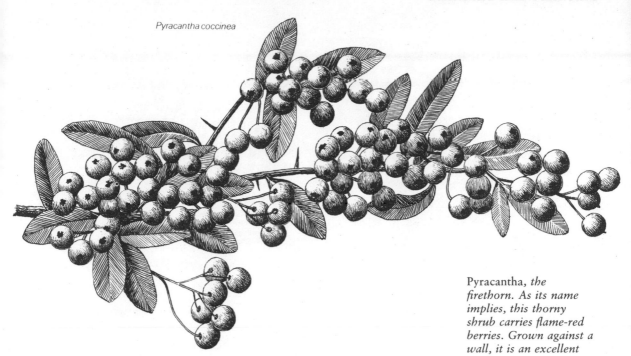

Pyracantha coccinea

Pyracantha, *the firethorn. As its name implies, this thorny shrub carries flame-red berries. Grown against a wall, it is an excellent nest site.*

at its margins, and robins, thrushes and blackbirds find insects and invertebrates under low-growing shrubs. Apart from birds, small mammals can travel through this sort of border without exposing themselves to danger, and away from a pond this is the most likely place to find a frog or toad.

Look in your garden centre for the low-growing varieties of *Berberis* and *Cotoneaster*. Periwinkle, which has purple flowers and is available in a variegated variety, and *Hypericum*, the Rose of Sharon, with yellow flowers, are both rapid colonizers of open ground, and will tolerate shade and clipping with shears when the need comes to keep them within bounds. Alternatives are *Euonymus radicans*, a low-growing version of the spindle, *Hebe* 'Carl Teschner', *Mahonia aquifolium*, and the

The rowan is an attractive, open tree. The red berries are a favourite of waxwings. Hawthorn, grown as a tree or hedge, provides unbeatable cover for nesting. Birds like the berries, too.

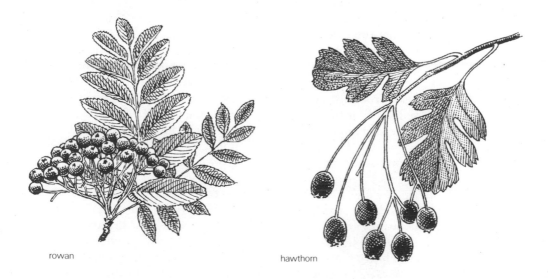

rowan

hawthorn

yew

The blooms of the flowering currant attract insects upon which birds feed. Later birds will eat the berries, too. The poisonous kernel of the yew berry passes harmlessly through the digestive system of the birds which eat it.

uncommon *Pachysandra*, which you may find in a nursery as Japanese spurge.

For sunny parts of the garden the heathers will cover the ground and provide a home for insects, in particular attracting bees when in flower, in the same way that thyme does. *Helianthemum*, which may be known as rock rose or sun rose, is another subject suitable for dry, sunny banks. It will flower from May to July if the flowers are dead-headed, and the soil is free-draining and unfertilized.

FLOWERS

The beauty and fragrance of flowers is not only attractive to us. It is the flower's means of attracting insects to it, so that fertilization takes place and seed is produced. It is not by chance that something as ostentatious as a sunflower is usually crowded with bees and hoverflies eager for its nectar, or that the powerful scent of honeysuckle on the night air will attract moths from all around. Apart from their value in bringing to your garden the insects on which birds feed, some flower seeds are eaten by birds. Greenfinches, tits and sparrows love sunflower seeds, and goldfinches will come for the seeds of aster, Michaelmas daisy, golden rod and poppy. Each year a charm of these delightful birds would come to my last garden for cornflower seeds, and there were always enough left to self-seed for the next year. At the same place I observed a small party of linnets feeding on the seed of *Alyssum* in the front garden, inches from the pavement. The same flower is much loved by insects, and gives off a very strong scent of honey.

In a large garden with mature trees, any of the umbellifers, from the smaller angelica, cow parsley and cow parsnip, to the giant hogweed, will provide spotted flycatchers with plentiful insect food. The seeds can be collected from roadside plants anywhere in Britain, but the giant hogweed should be avoided unless it is already growing in your garden. If it is, fence it off, since its hairy stem can cause a serious skin rash. Other species include meadowsweet, which likes damp ground, is also attractive to insects, and provides bullfinches with food in the form of its seeds. For butterflies, the iceplant (*Sedum spectabile*), Michaelmas daisies, and nettles are recommended. The nettles are not for the flowers but are the foodplant of red admiral, peacock, comma and small tortoiseshell butterfly caterpillars.

Of the typical border flowers, bullfinches like the seeds of forget-me-nots, wallflowers, snapdragons and pansies. They will also come to the seed-heads of thistles, although this is really goldfinch fare. Teasels, which also make attractive plant decorations and will grow from the seed of wild plants, are another of those native plants which feed insects when in flower and birds when seeded. This is true of most of our 'weeds', and also some grasses. It is noticeable that it is the long, flowering grasses that attract the blues and skippers, and indeed some grasses are the larval food of some of these butterflies. If you can afford to leave some of your lawn unmown until the grass has seeded, so much the better.

LAWNS

Lawns are relatively artificial habitats, having no real natural equivalent. Their nearest countryside equivalent is sheep pasture, which may attract rooks and starlings searching for leather-jackets, lapwings looking for small invertebrates, and in winter fieldfares and redwings among others. The garden lawn will be host to blackbirds and song thrushes looking for worms, dunnocks and chaffinches in search of smaller items of food, pied wagtails and spotted flycatchers catching insects on it, and it is the classic place to find a hoopoe, feeding up after overshooting on its northerly migration. This is not because hoopoes particularly like lawns, although they do prefer open ground for feeding, but because the hoopoe's barred plumage, so effective as camouflage in the dappled shade of an olive tree, makes the bird conspicuous when forced by hunger to feed on an open lawn!

With wildlife other than birds in mind, you might try letting some of your lawn grow long, around some daffodils set into the grass perhaps. Here some 'creepy-crawlies' may find refuge, butterflies will find nectar, and a frog can find moisture. If ants nest, you may find a green woodpecker on your lawn, catching them on the tip of its long, sticky tongue. If you have the space or the inclination, you could make a wild flower meadow, for which a number of seed mixes are now available commercially.

WATER

Water is essential to birds, as they must both drink and bathe. The most frequent visitors to drinking water are the seed eaters such as finches, for there is little moisture in the food they eat. Providing water is a good method of bringing hawfinches or crossbills to the garden, if there are some in the neighbourhood. Insect-eaters may need to drink less frequently, but they need to keep their feathers in trim just as much, and are more likely to be seen bathing.

The minimum that is required is an upturned dustbin lid set off the

Right: *An old dustbin lid is the simplest improvized drinking pool.*

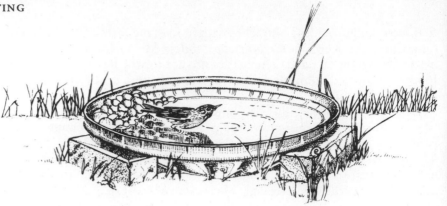

Below: *Oxygenating plants are an essential feature of a garden pond.*

Canadian pondweed

water violet

ground on bricks, or a small glass-fibre pool of the sort sold by the RSPB. In winter it can be kept ice-free by placing a night light underneath, out of a draught, or by submerging an aquarium immersion heater into the pool, covering this and its thermostat with gravel. If you don't do either in very cold weather it will mean repeated trips with hot water to unfreeze the birds' water supply. Similarly in dry weather one of these little pools will need constantly refilling, as a few energetic bathers will soon empty the pond. Site in an open situation, so the birds cannot be surprised by predators. A suitable perch nearby will allow the birds to check the area out before landing. Better still, because it will need less attention, and because it will support a plant or two, is an old rectangular stoneware sink. This should be deep enough to prevent it freezing solid, killing any life in it, but you must ensure that any creature that enters it can also get out. Some plant pots of varying sizes, with water-loving plants in, can be arranged to make steps out of the water. Frogs will frequently make their homes in such ponds, provided there is cover close by or a water lily to hide under.

PONDS

An ideal is the purpose-made pond, because it supports a whole range of wildlife which keeps it healthy, providing maintenance-free water for your birds in all but the driest, or coldest, weather. Siting is all important, as a shady pool can get clogged up with dropped leaves, which also reduce the oxygen content of the water. Excessive shade will also inhibit plant growth. As above, an intermediate perch between the pond and the nearest cover will allow your visitors to approach cautiously without putting them at risk from predators.

An essential feature of your pond, whether preformed glass-fibre, butyl-lined, or concrete, is that the ground slopes gently to its margins, so that you create shallow edges for the birds to enter the water, and shelves for your emergent plants. You must also have submergent plants – the 'weeds' that will keep your water aerated. These can be bought at garden centres or from pet shops, but better still get some from a friend whose own well-established pond needs some weeding. At the same time you can get a bucketful of their pond water, which should contain lots of goodies. Recommended aerators are hornworts and starworts, arrowhead, water violet and quillwort. These and the emergents – like reed-mace (bulrushes), rushes, irises and reeds – are best contained to prevent a total takeover. A small island or exposed rock could be introduced to create another safe place for wildlife. At the same time you can position any posts or perches you may want as an inducement for birds to come to

With a plastic lined pond (left) plenty of overlap is necessary as the weight of the water takes up a substantial amount of slack. Line the hole with old newspapers to prevent any sharp objects tearing the lining. Cover all the exposed edges with turf, soil or paving, as sunlight degrades the lining. Below is shown a pre-shaped glass-fibre pond.

Left and right: *Stages in planting a water lily in a basket.*

Below: *Profile showing the positions of oxygenating, floating and emergent water plants.*

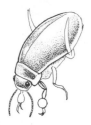

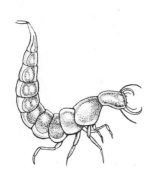

drink. The pond needs to be built to a depth of 45–60 cm (18–24 in) to ensure unfrozen water at all times.

Leave your new pond to settle for at least a week before introducing animal life. You will need some water snails (ram's horns or freshwater winkles) to help control algae, and maybe some fishes to graze the plants and provide food for kingfishers. Minnows and sticklebacks would be a good choice, provided they are only taken from a pond with a healthy stock, and with the owner's permission. The insect life that will colonize the pond will help to feed your fishes, and so will tadpoles. This is a good reason for keeping your fish stock low, and for avoiding goldfish which eat the young tadpoles. Other aquatic predators are the great diving beetle (and its larva), and the nymphs of dragonflies and damselflies. Unfortunately you can't have the beautiful adults without their fierce, highly predatory nymphal stages, and you will have to be patient and philosophical as they try and work their way through all the pond's other small livestock. At one pond at my place of work we have seen four newts – one we caught when we dipped the pond, one was the victim of a moorhen, which didn't even bother to eat it, one fell prey to the larva of a great diving beetle, and the last was taken by a blackbird! All of this was upsetting, but we couldn't interfere; we just hoped that the evidence indicated a healthy live newt population. Less harrowing, however, and demonstrating how subjective we are about predators and their prey, was the song thrush that fished for water snails on the margins of the pond, using the nearby paving slabs as an anvil.

MAINTENANCE IN THE GARDEN

However generous you are in letting nature take its course in your garden, some maintenance will be necessary. Grass will have to be mown, some pruning undertaken, fallen leaves collected and even some weeding will be inevitable, especially in the early years. The waste from these operations has to go somewhere, and you will need to plan for a compost heap and also for somewhere to burn some of the woodier waste. Even if you make cuttings from most of your prunings, you still need to dispose of diseased wood and weeds whose seeds will survive the composting process. In my relatively large garden (21 × 14 m/70 × 45 ft, plus yard) I still find that I haven't the space to light a bonfire without scorching something, so I have an incinerator instead. The fine ash produced is mixed with compost and goes back on to the garden.

Two carnivorous aquatic insects you may find in your pond. From top to bottom: the female, male and larva of the great diving beetle; and a waterboatman, showing under view and top view.

The compost heap is another of the garden's self-contained eco-systems, where bacteria and fungi break down vegetable matter into a humus rich in nutrients. The essentials for composting are air, moisture and heat, and of course the organisms that break down the plant cellulose by aerobics. Nitrogen speeds up the process, and is readily available in animal manure.

Unless you have lots of space, you will need to contain your compost. A container bin can be purchased or you can make your own, but the principle remains the same. The base needs to have air flowing under it, and ideally the sides, too, should allow air to circulate. The front, or part of it should be removable, so that you can get at your compost. Heat will build up in the vegetable matter, and a plastic sheet over the top of your

None of these waterbirds is a true garden species, but all will take advantage of ready food supplies. Top and below: grey heron; centre: female mallard with chicks; bottom left: moorhen; bottom right: male and female mallard.

29

Right: *The kestrel is our only bird of prey to habitually hover, head down into the wind, searching the ground for prey.*

Below: *As with most birds of prey, a female sparrowhawk is noticeably larger than her mate. They are becoming more frequent in built-up areas.*

♂

♀

Right: *A pair of kestrels tend their young (the male is on the right). They may use the old nest of a crow, a ledge on a building or cliff, or a hole in a tree.*

Opposite: *At close range a sparrowhawk's eye is a glaring yellow. They sometimes visit bird feeding stations to prey on small birds. In woodland, blue tits are a major food item.*

Gulls thrive on the waste we produce. Black-headed gulls (bottom) in particular are city-dwellers outside the breeding season, and often visit gardens. The gull in flight on the right is a herring gull.

summer

herring gull

winter

winter

summer

juvenile

black-headed gull

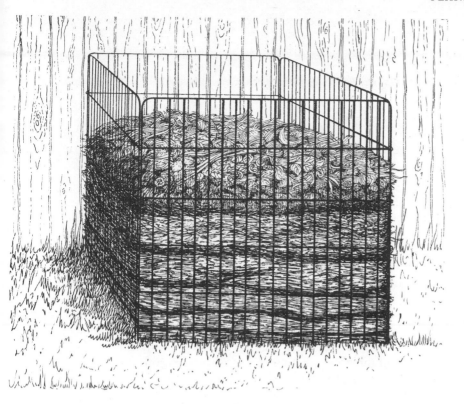

An open wire container allows air to circulate freely, aiding the composting process. Cover the top of the heap in very dry, or very wet, weather.

heap will prevent it drying out or getting too wet, both of which will inhibit the aerobic process.

All your garden refuse except seeding weeds and woody or diseased cuttings can go on the heap, and kitchen waste like potato peelings can, too. Grass cuttings produce a great deal of heat and break down fast, but leaves take much longer. A few can go to the compost heap, but large quantities should be stacked in a wire mesh container and spread around the base of your shrubs the following autumn. The birds will find plenty of invertebrates there during the winter.

A leaf pile like this is an ideal place for a hedgehog to hibernate – as is a bonfire in autumn – so take care! Grass snakes may choose a compost heap in which to lay their eggs, leaving the heat generated inside the heap to incubate the eggs. Anyone finding such a nest should feel very privileged, and leave the eggs undisturbed to hatch. Grass snakes are quite harmless to man, though their food may include young birds. But the birds will benefit from your compost heap, too. Break it open on a frosty day, and a robin is guaranteed to come for the plentiful worms and other invertebrates that live there. Thrushes, redwings, fieldfares and black-birds will also partake. Spread your compost in mid-winter, and let the birds help to break open any lumps as they search for food. Later, as the soil temperature warms up, the worms will finish the job for you, dragging the humus into the soil below. Ideally you need two compost heaps, so that you can keep a cycle going.

Near to your compost heap, or in the wild patch if you have one, you can leave some timber to rot. Introduce a decaying (but not diseased) branch from your local wood and you will also add to the garden menagerie.

House sparrows in particular like to dust-bathe.

Another feature that you may prefer to tuck away in this area, although you will miss some fun if you do, is a dust bowl for sparrows and wrens. Partridges and pheasants also dust bathe, and the country garden could witness a fine cock pheasant at its toilet! All you need is an 0.6 × 0.3 m (2 × 1 ft) area of finely sieved sand, earth and ash, a few centimetres deep.

In developing your garden there may be some casualties, but by treating your prunings as cuttings you should have a well-stocked nursery to replace any failures. Regular pruning is not necessary on most shrubs grown for berries, but some will have to be pruned, if only to assist their less vigorous neighbours. In order to keep the supply of berries, prune on a three-year cycle. Excess stock can be given to friends to encourage their bird-gardening, or swapped for plants you need. My neighbour's ash tree keeps me constantly supplied with seedlings which I give away in the hope that they will reach maturity elsewhere, contributing to the health of the environment outside the garden.

So much of what we do in the bird-garden has this spin-off. Birds, butterflies and insects are all highly mobile, and our efforts in encouraging these forms of life may lead to colonizations elsewhere. Less mobile creatures like frogs and hedgehogs also benefit, and it may be in years to come, that it is garden-bred animals like these that act as a reservoir, repopulating the countryside in a more enlightened era. Combined, we may have an influence far greater than our individual land holdings suggest.

BIRD GARDENING WITH CHILDREN

What about the bird-gardener with a growing family? The requirements of children and birds are not the same, but with care the two can be compatible. The answer is long-term planning with the needs of children considered early on. Let's consider the children first. Their prime requirements are a grassy playing area and some hard surface for using bicycles, etc. in wet weather. Both these features will also provide places where birds can feed, but whereas children's games need fairly large expanses of ground without obstructions, birds like perching posts and cover.

Depending on the size of your garden, the lawn may have to remain tree-less, to give your children the space they need. But the larger your garden, the more opportunity to introduce trees and shrubs to the lawn and its borders. As long as they are not fragile specimens they can soon become part of the children's play: becoming 'home' in games of chase, or base for a 'camp'. If a tree in the lawn is going to get damaged or simply be in the way, then plan to plant one when the children are older and their need for limitless space is less.

The same sort of ground rules will apply to the hard playing area. A planted feature in the centre of some paving will create a circuit for the children to ride round. Why not plant a buddleia? Once the youngsters have enjoyed the butterflies it attracts they will recognize the value of the plant and cherish it. The same will apply to a rowan tree, a sunflower or some Michaelmas daisies.

If you have space, let your children have their own garden. Sunflowers are easily grown (although they may need staking), look spectacular and attract insect and bird life. A few of these, and some smaller flowers like *Alyssum* and cornflowers that will attract wildlife, will soon convince children that they have a part to play in the wildlife garden.

What about poisonous berries? Berry-bearing shrubs are a must for the bird garden, and few berries are lethal. Those that will attract birds but should not be encouraged are woody and deadly nightshades, black and white bryony, *Laburnum*, spindle, *Convolvulus* and yew. *Convolvulus* (bindweed), is worth eradicating anyhow as it strangles anything it climbs up, unlike the much maligned ivy (which is also poisonous). Most of the rest are probably sufficiently unpleasant to taste (I haven't tried them) to stop children eating more than one berry, which is unlikely to cause more than a slight stomach upset. If you feel you can't trust your child not to eat berries, then don't plant berry producers. You will have to provide only bird table food until your children are older.

Being prepared to wait may also apply to a garden pond. However, you could start with an 'elephant's foot', which is a fibre-glass drinking trough. Even this will bring birds to drink and bathe, and it can be camouflaged easily enough. Later you could start with a small, shallow pond which can be linked to a larger, deeper pond in due course.

Perhaps teaching respect for a wild patch is the most difficult task with young children. Let them have a 'camp' smack in the middle of it, with a few well-defined routes leading in and out. This way the children will want to preserve the high vegetation as much as you do, because it provides concealment. Of course if the children are very noisy there will be no birds in the garden, but I've frequently observed birds feeding when the kids are more quietly absorbed, and have even seen a blackbird share a shower when the children were playing under a hose during a hot, dry spell.

In winter encourage your offspring to put out food for the birds, and see how possessive they become when something lands on 'their' piece of bird-cake. Similarly they can be involved with building and siting nest boxes.

Although the child's natural eagerness may cause a few problems, their interest and involvement will lead to a care and respect for all forms of life in the garden, making each stage in the conversion to a wildlife garden progressively easier.

By pruning on a four-year cycle you can produce flowering and fruiting wood without the shrub growing out of bounds.

3rd year

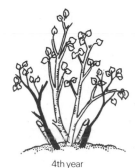

4th year

5th year

subsequent years

35

Feeding garden birds

'The north wind doth blow, and we shall have snow, and what shall poor Robin do then, poor thing!' Even the well-stocked bird garden is going to be a fairly harsh place in which to live during the depths of winter. During the worst of our winter weather, patches of ground will usually remain open in a woodland, where the mass of trunks and branches will create swirls and eddies that influence where the snow falls. In the leaf litter robins, blackbirds and chaffinches search for food to sustain them through the long winter nights. In gardens, it is only under the largest shrubs that there is likely to be free ground, but even then unless there is some humus present the soil will be hard and inhospitable.

Arguably, without feeding, a higher proportion of garden birds than those dwelling in woodland would die in winter. In reality, the situation is probably the reverse. The millions who feed birds, plus the slightly higher winter temperatures to be found in our big conurbations, combine to bring mortality down to quite low levels. During a big freeze even skylarks will enter gardens in search of food, and I remember in the very cold winter of 1981/2 a fieldfare feeding on a tiny scrap of grass by a main road in a town, and a meadow pipit searching the soiled snow on a pavement for food. Seeing a robin on the snow, many people's first instinct will be to throw it some crumbs, and for some people feeding the birds stops there. Throwing out some bread may bring you house sparrows, starlings and feral pigeons, but with an assortment of foods and feeding stations you can increase the numbers and varieties of birds in your garden enormously. Even if you have no garden, you can still feed the birds by using your window sill. It is possible to purchase a little device that can be fixed to a window ledge and which has a compartment for food, and one for water. A similar one that has suckers for sticking directly on to a window is also available. Make sure your window is clean and dry, and create the vacuum you need by smearing a little household lubricating oil round the inside of the suction cup. There is also a window attachment to enable you to suspend a spiral feeder from your window which, when filled with peanuts, is a great favourite with tits.

BIRD TABLES

If you have a garden, you will probably want to erect a bird table. This is a practical way of providing a safe place for most garden birds to feed, but it is important to remember that some birds prefer to feed on the ground, and should also be catered for.

A ground feeding tray is really just a bird table on the ground. It should have a 2.5 cm (1 in) high lip all round, with a 2.5 cm (1 in) gap at each corner to allow water to drain away. Ideally you should mount this on castors, which will lift it off the grass and allow you to move it fractionally each time you put out food so that no part of the lawn suffers. This has another advantage, because if the bird tray is static the ground around will gradually become fouled with droppings, with the attendant risk of disease. For the same reason it is advisable to clean any sort of feeder from time to time, and to alter their positions periodically.

Maintenance is best carried out in autumn, before the harsh weather of winter. After a thorough clean, wooden items can be treated with a preservative, which should be given plenty of time to dry thoroughly before they are used. Loose screws should be tightened or replaced, when galvanized screws can be substituted for any rusting ones. The means by which you hang any devices should be checked to ensure they are secure, and indeed all your bird-feeding equipment surveyed for anything that may put the birds at risk. This is also a good time to take stock and consider whether any of your equipment, or its siting, could be improved, for the birds' comfort and your pleasure.

There are plenty of bird table designs available, and many of these have roofs. This is regarded as an affectation by some, but it does keep the food dry in wet weather and affords the birds some protection as they feed, from both rain and sparrowhawks. Most of the commercially produced tables, whether covered or not, can be fixed to a post (about 1.2 m/4 ft above the ground), or suspended at a similar height.

Hanging the bird table near the tip of a branch or making a gallows-like construction from which to suspend it will have some advantages if it deters cats or squirrels from gaining access to the table top. The presence of cats is also a reason for siting your bird table where the birds will have a clear line of vision, so that they can see danger easily. Birds like to approach their food cautiously, so a high bush or tree nearby will make an ideal perch from which to scan the area before coming to feed. If you only have a small yard, a washing line will be just as useful as a perch (or for hanging the feeder from). Your visitors will also use these perches in order

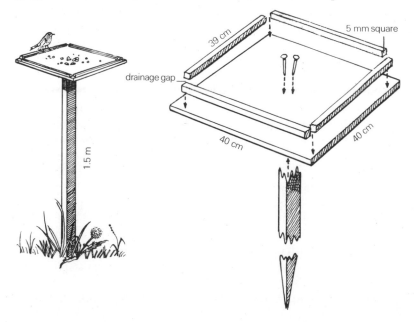

39 cm

5 mm square

drainage gap

40 cm

40 cm

1.5 m

A bird table can be constructed quite cheaply and simply. The harmful chemicals present in most wood preservatives should be given time to evaporate before use.

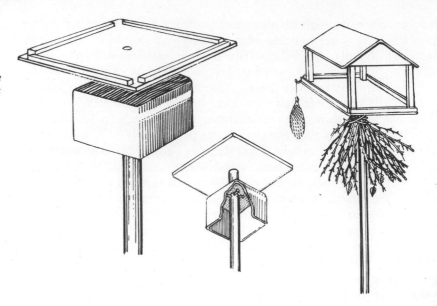

to queue up before they feed, because there is a 'pecking-order' both among birds of the same type and between the species, which means there are always some individuals that will have to wait their turn. Watching the bird table to find the most dominant species and individuals can be fascinating, and may give you ideas as to how you can provide for the less assertive species (see the chapter on Birdwatching).

To return to the problem of cats and squirrels, a first line in the defence of feeding tables is to use a smooth metal or plastic-covered pole. On a wooden post an inverted metal cone will act as a deterrent, while more natural measures include training a climbing rose up the post or tying a bundle of twigs (facing downward so that the lower end is wider than the upper) of rose, gorse or holly to the post. At least one manufacturer produces a feeder that combines a slim plastic pole with a circular tray, the centre of which is a water compartment. Water really is as essential in winter as it is in summer, and should always be provided along with the food. A little grit can also be given with the food, to be picked up as the birds feed, just as they do naturally. This helps them digest the food, by grinding the food up in the gizzard. In very cold weather when the ground is frozen or snow covered the birds may find their natural supply is not available to them. In order to conserve supplies of grit – the sort sold for cage birds is perfectly adequate – it is best to dispense it from a seed hopper, which is a pretty good way of putting out seed, too! The seed is gravity fed from a V-shaped container into a tray at the base so that, although the supply is maintained, the excess that can be scattered is kept to a minimum. On the covered table previously mentioned there are slides provided for a hopper which fits neatly under the roof.

Some bird feeders are designed entirely on the hopper principle, with the birds perching on the rim of the food tray which avoids fouling the food with their droppings, while others incorporate a low conical roof which keeps the food dry. Another bird table design separates off an area of the bird table by using a mesh to create a cage which smaller birds can freely enter, leaving some of the aggressive species like starlings and blackbirds outside. To be avoided are those rustic-looking bird tables so beloved of some garden centres which incorporate a nest hole in the gable, too! The rough timber gives a good foothold to predators, the untreated wood has a short life once the bark has gone, and inviting birds to feed by another's nest site is calculated to produce neurosis!

HANGING FEEDERS

Because of the different ways in which birds feed, and their various levels of tolerance of other birds feeding nearby, it is a good idea to provide a variety of feeding devices. Hanging feeders are easily positioned around the garden, and can even be hung from the bird table itself.

The most straightforward hanging device is the red mesh bag, filled with peanuts. This will certainly encourage a prompt visit from our most common tits, and is also likely to be visited by house sparrows and greenfinches. The greatest thrill, however, is when some siskins discover your nutbag, as they are quite likely to if there are alders, birches or conifers nearby. At my office, where we feed birds this way outside the

A wide variety of feeding devices is now available from a number of sources. From left to right: hanging bird table with seed hopper; spiral peanut feeder; wire food basket; peanut kebab.

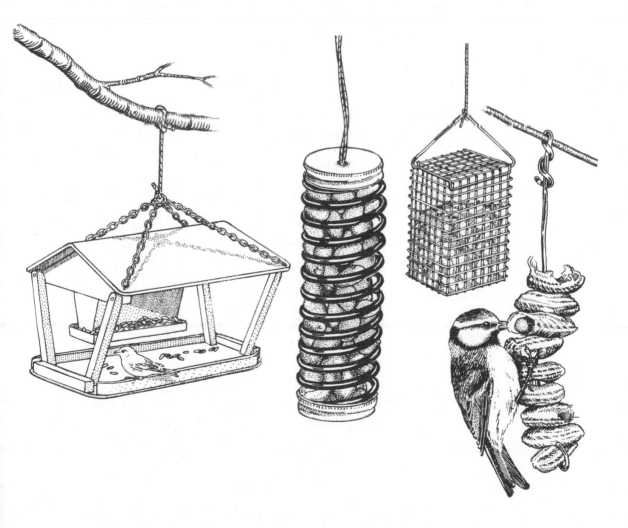

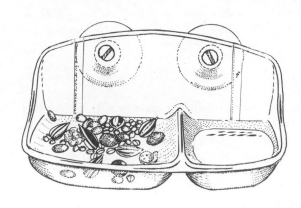

Two types of clear plastic food dispensers. The one on the left allows the birds to climb inside to feed, and the one on the right can be attached to a window.

RECIPE FOR BIRD PUDDING

Take roughly equal parts of the following:

*broken biscuits
dry cake
dried fruits
chopped fresh fruit
seed
peanuts
oatmeal
crumbs
cereal dust
cheese*

Mix well. Place in half-coconut shell or tit bell, about two-thirds full. Pour hot (melted) fat over the mixture to the top and leave to set. Hang receptacle upside down, outside.

windows, it is not unusual to have four or five different species on the bag at a time, and as many as seven individuals. Although siskins rarely come when other species are feeding, they are quite aggressive and this is not always the case. Occasionally a robin has paid a brief visit, and a nutbag of this sort hung from a tree and filled with suet tempted a great spotted woodpecker to come and feed during a period when snow was on the ground.

Similar to the mesh bag is a plastic-coated wire-mesh cage, about the size of a mug, which can be filled with a variety of foods. Being of more rigid design it enables the less agile birds like starlings to feed, so if you want to exclude them you really need something that is only open at the base. Half a coconut suspended upside down is the most 'basic model', but you will have to position the hole accurately or it will hang lopsided. A tit bell, made of ceramic or wood, is a more sophisticated version of this, but you will have to make a bird pudding in order to fill it. Bird pudding contains any food that is normally offered, minced up and bound together with fat which is poured over the mixture when hot. Of course you can make the pudding in your own mould, using string rather like a candle wick so that you can suspend the pudding when set. The benefit of providing a pudding rather than loose food is that it encourages the birds to feed where the food is provided, rather than taking it away and storing it as coal tits are likely to do. Another version of the coconut-type feeder is a wooden box with a mesh base, which hinges open to allow the box to be filled. This has the same advantages as the tit bell, but needs to be filled with loose food.

The most sophisticated hanging feeders are made of clear acrylic, and have all the advantages of that material, but personally I find their appearance in the garden incongruous. One is a globe which is filled from the top, with three holes in the lower half where the birds gain access to the food. It seems to be used most by the tits, which either perch on the rim of the hole or enter the globe itself, where they can be seen through the acrylic happily feeding under cover. The other acrylic feeder is a cylinder with holes at intervals in the sides, each with a perch. The top comes off to fill it, and has a handle from which to hang it. The poor man's version of this is a straight branch with the side shoots left on to provide perches. By each perch a hole is drilled which is then stuffed with nuts or filled with

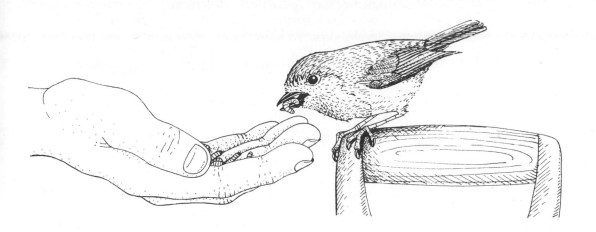

fat. The branch has a hook attached at one end and the whole is hung from a tree. This is a variation of the photographer's trick of baiting a natural feeding perch like a log with fat placed in pre-drilled holes, or mealworms or peanuts pushed into the crevices. The photograph only shows the bird and its perch, although there are often tell-tale pieces of food on the bird's bill to give the game away!

Robins are one of the easier subjects to train to feed from the hand.

Most of the previously mentioned feeders can be made at home with a little care and imagination, but do think of the welfare of your visitors and avoid any sharp edges or springy parts that could trap a bird's leg. For this reason you should never try to make a home-made version of the spiral feeder, as sold by the RSPB. Their version is quite rigid, although the shape may at first sight suggest that it is springy, and both ends have an aluminium screw-on cap. The do-it-yourself version here is the peanut kebab, in which a whole row of nuts are skewered on to a length of wire, and one end is bent over to form a hook. The other must be sharp enough to pierce the nuts, so when your kebab is complete cap the sharp end with a rubber, plasticene or similar, which will also stop the peanuts falling off. (You will probably find, however, that great tits have a fondness for rubber, just as they do for putty!)

FEEDING FROM THE HAND

Before taming a bird to feed from your hand, do consider any risk you may cause the bird by encouraging it to trust humans or come very close to a house. Having said that, it is almost invariably the case that a tamed bird will only come to the person who regularly feeds it. (The exceptions to this are the feral pigeons, house sparrows and other birds which have become so accustomed to being fed in town parks that they are virtually unafraid of man.)

In the majority of gardens a robin may be the best subject for hand feeding. They can be very confiding, practically getting under your boots to search for worms in freshly dug soil, so that all that is required is slow and deliberate movements, offering them cheese or their favourite – mealworms – first on the ground close to you, until gradually you entice the bird on to your hand. This may take days or months, but the key words are patience and regularity. Cold weather will certainly make birds bolder, and this could be a good time to start. If you are feeding from a window ledge, leave the window open a little, approaching nearer day by day until you are seated right by the open window. If the birds still remain unconcerned, rest your hand on the window ledge with some food on it, allowing the birds to treat your hand like any other receptacle. In time the hand with food on it will be regarded in the same way as a dish of food being proffered.

REGULARITY

If you are going to feed birds on a regular basis, then you really must commit yourself to carry on throughout the winter because your regular visitors will become quite dependent on you as a source of food. Without the food you have provided they would have foraged far afield, possibly flocking with their own kind or even joining in mixed flocks in search of food. To cut off their supply of food in hard weather would almost certainly mean they would starve before finding alternative supplies. The example of the ring-necked parakeet illustrates the point. These birds have established feral populations in the south-east of England, in Merseyside and in Greater Manchester, originating from escaped aviary birds. There is little doubt that the success of the ring-necked parakeets in surviving our winters is due to garden feeding, where they are fond of peanuts and various fruits. Forty-five per cent of records for these aggressive feeders come from gardens, and the population is now about 500 pairs. Ring-necked parakeets have recently been accepted on to the British List. By contrast the feral budgerigars on Tresco in the Isles of Scilly seem to have died out, presumably because there were not sufficient people feeding them through the winter.

Putting food out first thing in the morning and again in mid-afternoon will benefit the birds most. This replenishes them after the night when they expend enormous amounts of energy simply keeping warm, and fuels them up again at the end of the day before they go to roost. Most birds need to increase their body weight by about one-third to cope with the demands of winter and, having achieved this, they must maintain the extra fat reserves while feeding time is drastically reduced. To cope with this birds like wrens and pied wagtails need to feed almost continuously throughout the daylight hours in order not to lose any weight.

It is strange then that these two birds – both common and widely distributed – are not more regular bird table users, and one can only come to the conclusion that it is their timidity in relation to other birds, rather than a fear of man, that keeps them away. The British Trust for Ornithology's Garden Bird Feeding Study showed that they came to 44.9 per cent (pied wagtail) and 33.6 per cent (wren) of the feeding stations contributing to the survey. By comparison, the 'top nine' visitors were all recorded at over 90 per cent of feeding stations. They were, in order: blackbird, blue tit, robin, house sparrow, starling, dunnock, great tit, chaffinch and greenfinch. The blackbird had a 99.3 per cent visit rating, while the tenth bird in the rankings, the song thrush, recorded 88.4 per cent. Not surprisingly the most numerous, as opposed to most frequent visitors, were house sparrows and starlings.

All this serves to illustrate the importance of where you put your food. Some birds, like the blackbird, seem to be at home either on a bird table or on the ground. Dunnocks and chaffinches prefer to feed on what has been spilled from the table, while the agile tits will hang upside down from feeders in order to get their share. Interestingly our most numerous bird table visitors prefer to feed a little further away from the window than do some of the less assertive birds, and it has been suggested that if you want to discourage the starlings and sparrows it may be worth providing them with their own table further away from the house. It is also true that these two will feed quite happily on bread, whereas their less aggressive cousins are more particular in their tastes. This doesn't mean of course that the sparrows and starlings won't eat the other bird's preferred food – they will – but it does give an idea of the subtleties of bird feeding.

TYPES OF FOOD

The wider the range of foods provided, the greater the variety of birds you can expect to visit your garden. While most garden birds feed their young on insects and themselves eat other invertebrates during the warmer part of the year, the majority become more catholic in their tastes in winter, and most will accept a wide variety of food. Nevertheless it is still those foods which are closer to an animal diet, with a high fat content, which are taken by the greatest numbers of birds. Thus peanuts, suet, fat and cheese will appeal to most of your potential visitors. It is worth experimenting, though, because you are quite likely to find that the less common visitors have more specialized tastes, and may become regular visitors to one kind of food only.

BREAD, POTATO AND RICE
Bread is bird food at its most basic, and is probably the favourite of no individual species, although a number will take it. Its value is increased if it is rubbed vigorously between the palms to crumb it, ensuring that all get a fair share. (The wholemeal types are more beneficial than the basic white variety.) Dunnocks and pied wagtails will pick up the tiniest crumbs from the ground after the other species have abandoned the bird table. Potatoes should be served baked in their jackets and will occupy blackbirds and starlings among others. Rice, that other great staple, is not generally recommended, because like other dried foods it will tend to swell up in the crop of the bird when moist. Although wild birds in India and China doubtless take rice seed from plants growing in paddyfields, it is only cooked rice, for instance from a leftover rice pudding, that is really safe to offer.

GRAIN
Grain-based foods, like biscuits and cake, are perfectly suitable, but again are not the favourite food of any bird, nor especially nutritious. Their ideal use would be in a bird pudding, which tits will devour with gusto when hung in a tit bell, with blackbirds and thrushes picking up the fallen bits from the ground.

Pure grain in the form of wheat and barley is a favourite of gamebirds, as anyone who lives in pheasant-rearing country will know. Where grain is left for pheasants in an open ride it is not unusual to put up flocks of sixty-plus birds, including tree sparrows, greenfinches and perhaps the

Different bill shapes have evolved to cope with differing foods.

treecreeper (probing bark)

nuthatch (general-purpose insect and nut-eater)

swift (catching insects in flight)

great tit (insects and seeds)

spotted flycatcher (hovers, catching insects in flight)

43

The seed eaters have quite stout bills, each adapted to its particular job.

goldfinch (probing seeds of thistles)

hawfinch (cracking nuts)

chaffinch (general-purpose seeds)

bullfinch (tearing open seeds)

crossbill (opening pine cones to reach seeds)

odd brambling, when they are disturbed. Other regulars at these sites are collared doves, feral pigeons, moorhens and mallards, any of which might be enticed into a country garden by the lure of grain. Another infrequent visitor to the garden that may be drawn by grain is the partridge, particularly if the food were near a boundary hedge bordering open country.

I've often wondered how birds come to locate food supplies as quickly as they do, and can only conclude that there is a vast traffic of birds outside the breeding season that is largely unnoticed until they home in on food. Certainly on the occasions I have spent a whole day at home gardening, I have been aware of such birds as redpolls flying over calling to each other, small parties of skylarks with their characteristic contact calls, and one spring a great spotted woodpecker plying a regular route from a well-wooded garden nearby. Presumably had any of these seen a likely source of food they would have dropped in to investigate. A bird like a partridge will probably only come into a garden early in the morning when everything is quiet, and if it finds nothing will move on, leaving us none the wiser.

SEED

Seeds are, of course, the main diet of finches and buntings, and can be offered as mixed seed bought by the packet or in bulk, or native seeds that have been collected in autumn in the countryside. The commercial mixes which can be obtained from pet shops, by mail order or from corn merchants, have mainly imported seed in them, but this doesn't seem to bother the finches. As stated earlier, the best way to dispense seed is from a hopper, but in hard weather when your regular greenfinches and chaffinches may be joined by bramblings, spread some on the ground. If any happens to germinate the following spring you can simply harvest the seed after flowering.

A common seed in any mix is sunflower, which is easily collected from garden plants. Be sure to leave some plants intact, however, because you will derive much pleasure from watching the great tits, greenfinches, and sparrows feeding from the plants. Most other seeds are not so easy to collect in quantity, the best method being to cut the stem and bundle a few together, hanging them upside in a dry place with the seed heads in a bag (not polythene). Thistles, dock, teasel, ragwort and honesty give the best yield.

Berries can also be harvested and stored in a dry, dark place after drying in a tray. Alternatively they can be kept in the deep-freeze until needed. Berries from any of the shrubs mentioned in the last chapter will do, as well as crab apples and the fruit of the bird cherry. While you're collecting nuts to plant, you could also collect them for winter feeding. Whole nuts can be wedged in natural crevices all over the garden, but those on the bird table are best opened. Nuthatches and woodpeckers are the most likely to benefit from your labours here.

PEANUTS

Although Brazil nuts and other exotic Christmas varieties are as acceptable as home-grown hazels or walnuts, peanuts are bird food par excellence. They seem to have an almost universal appeal, and are easily dispensed without time consuming opening. Peanuts can be offered in their shells, of course, and provide great entertainment as great tits, nuthatches and coal tits attempt to find a way into them. In a freeze-up,

Coal tits are one of a number of species that will store food.

however, it may be kinder – and cheaper – to dispense shelled nuts bought in bulk, as a lot of energy goes into breaking open a nut. Hung in a mesh bag you can expect the peanuts to be eaten very quickly, especially if jays take to feeding on them, as the bag is likely to get torn. Then those great hoarders, the coal tits, will carry off whole nuts to store until the bag is empty. Sturdier devices for dispensing peanuts have already been described but the red mesh bag is still the most successful way of tempting siskins to your windows.

FRUIT

Don't throw away your windfalls! The surest way of pulling the winter thrushes into the garden is to distribute apples and pears when the hard frosts and snow of the new year arrive. Assuming you haven't the space to freeze a season's crop, the best way to store is as berries above. Distributed widely over the back of the lawn, or even under shrubs, you will help the redwings, fieldfares, thrushes and blackbirds to get through this most difficult part of the year. Really hard weather could attract very large numbers of birds, so eke out your stock with care so as not to leave the birds unprovided for. Dried fruit can be put out on to the bird table, too, after soaking. This seems to be one of the favoured foods of overwintering blackcaps, another phenomenon that has doubtless been initiated and then reinforced by the practice of feeding birds through the winter.

MEATS

Leave a dog's bone out in the garden and it doesn't take long for the starlings and house sparrows to find it. Leave it out all night and you may have a fox, or far less desirable, rats. Cooked meats on the bone are best therefore put on to a bird table or hung well out of reach of mammals. Tits in particular will appreciate this, and may be joined by a woodpecker. Crows will also come for meat, but may find a hanging bone a bit tricky. Jackdaws are the most frequent member of the crow family to come to garden feeders, ranking just after wrens in frequency of visits. Magpies are nearly as regular, rooks a little less so. Once in the garden they will eat anything, however, their presence being unsettling for the smaller birds. Being wary of man, they are not very keen to come for food put out close to a window.

Magpies have become numerous in some suburban areas over the last decade or so, becoming most obvious in spring when they raid the nests of songbirds for their eggs and young. This is no more pleasant to watch than the death of a newt described earlier, but like that incident it reflects a healthy population of the things on which magpies feed. If there is an abundance of magpies, it is because there is an abundance of songbirds, too, and the food they like to eat. It could be that the feeding of garden birds has enabled unusually high numbers of small birds to survive in the suburban environment, and the magpies have 'cashed in' on this. Short of shooting magpies – which would only be legal if the bird was on your property and the firearm was discharged no less than 15 m (50 ft) from the middle of the nearest road, putting nobody at risk – the only answer is to stop feeding birds. This would have to be done on an enormous scale to be effective, and is impractical. In my view it is also unnecessary, because if the magpies depressed the population of songbirds significantly, they would be forced out of the area themselves. If the numbers of songbirds remain buoyant, we can hardly protest that the magpies are doing any lasting harm.

The only alternative which removes the need to kill anything is to prevent magpies from nesting by destroying their nests while they are being built. Again it must be stressed that this is only legal if you own the land where the nest is being built, or have been authorized by the owner to do so. Reaching the nest is likely to prove difficult anyway, as magpies tend to build high or in the middle of a hawthorn. Frankly, I think we have to allow Nature to achieve a balance in a slightly unnatural situation.

FAT

Lumps of suet or fatty pieces from cooked meat can be put into a wire mesh cage and hung up for all sorts of birds to peck at. As with meat, woodpeckers and nuthatches are very partial to fat, as are the tits. Large pieces of fat on the bird table may simply be carried off by the larger birds, or attract cats, and cutting up small pieces can prove difficult. Dripping fat can be poured when hot over suitable surfaces like the top of a log, and allowed to congeal. Similarly it can be thrown on to the leaf litter under shrubs, so that it scatters, leaving tiny droplets which wrens and dunnocks may find. The other use for it is as a binder for bird pudding, described earlier. The ratio should be roughly two parts of the ingredients to one of fat.

LIVE FOOD

Apart from any fish unwittingly given to a heron or kingfisher, suitable live food is likely to be limited to mealworms, the robin's favourite. These are not the gentles that anglers use as bait, but the larvae of a beetle. Also unlike anglers' gentles they are not smelly. They can be purchased from some pet shops, but if you have a corner of a shed or greenhouse where you could breed them, you could have a continuous supply.

SOME FEEDING TIPS

Avoid salted food, like salted peanuts and salted bacon rind. It is harmful to birds since they cannot pass it easily through their systems. Dried food should always be soaked thoroughly so that it doesn't swell up in the bird's crop, but desiccated coconut should always be avoided. Peel from orange and lemons and banana skins should also not be offered. Don't encourage birds to a bird feeder if they are going to be put at risk from cats or other predators, and don't start feeding and then discontinue when the birds have become accustomed to being fed. Never add glycerine, alcohol, or anti-freeze to water to stop it freezing, as it will wreak havoc with their plumage if they bathe in it, resulting in almost certain death from chilling, and do untold harm if it is swallowed. Finally, don't feed between the months of April and November, with the exceptions described on page 48 under summer feeding.

MEALWORM CULTURE

Half fill a container – an earthenware jar or biscuit tin is best – with a mixture of bran, dried bread and biscuit, and introduce your mealworms, grubs and adult beetles, purchased from the petshop. Cover the top of your jar with a cloth, which should be kept moist with a squirt from a plant spray once a week. Add a little more of the same food each week (about a handful) and keep between 24–29°C (75–85°F). The adults live for about ten weeks, during which time a female may lay 600 eggs, each taking eight to ten days to hatch. You then have six months to feed them to the birds before they pupate, although you must allow some to mature in order to keep the culture growing. Mealworms are certainly the best way to tame a robin, and are also effective as bait for photography. When you're not hand-feeding robins or taking photographs you can also use your mealworms to clean up bird skulls you have found and may wish to preserve.

Live food, such as mealworms, will attract a variety of 'softbills'. This form of food is suitable for summer feeding.

SUMMER FEEDING

If, as I have suggested, the practice of feeding garden birds in winter lowers their mortality, with more birds surviving through to the following spring, aren't we obliged to carry on feeding them in the same way to maintain the extra numbers we have helped through the winter? I think the simple answer is no, for a number of reasons.

Firstly, as the days lengthen, the birds that thronged the bird table begin to disperse, pair off and establish territories. Generally, these territories are only defended against rivals of the same species, but occasionally other birds that are perceived as competitors for food or nest sites will also be driven away. An amazing variety of birds are able to live in close proximity to each other without conflict, because of their subtly different feeding habits and nesting requirements, but inevitably some birds remain unpaired and are forced to move away. Others, the less dominant or inexperienced, will pair but only find somewhere to nest on the margins of their ideal niche, and their attempts to breed will fail, because their nest site was unsuitable or there was insufficient food for the young. So Nature redresses the balance, and the artificially high population of birds disperses.

Secondly, in spring most of our garden birds turn to insect food – there aren't many seeds available anyway – and feed their young on caterpillars, earthworms, the larvae of beetles and flies, and flying insects. We are simply not capable of supplying sufficient food of the right kind at this time of the year. If we offer alternatives, we are likely to cause the deaths of as many nestlings as we save.

But we can do something positive if we have planned the garden well. All that careful planting and provision of cover pays off when we create nest sites by careful planning and the provision of nest boxes. All those hungry nestlings are fed because of the multitude of insects drawn to our gardens by the flowering shrubs and native plants we have encouraged. If the spring is dry and leads to a dry June, keep a supply of worms for the thrushes by watering your lawn and keeping the ground underneath soft. Keep a patch of earth well dug, whether you need it or not, and plunge a fork into the compost heap every now and then to expose new areas to the birds. When you're in the garden turn over a stone or log to help a robin get at some nice, juicy bug you've just revealed. And keep a plentiful supply of water available for drinking and bathing.

The only time that artificial feeding will really help is if there is a prolonged spell of cold, wet weather. Then some mealworms, grated cheese or suet dispensed in such a way that a parent bird cannot offer its young great choking lumps of the stuff may help the birds through this difficult time. Decrease the supplies gradually as the weather improves and you notice more insects on the wing. Soon the first fruits will be ripening and weeds will start to set seed, and the insect population reaches a peak. The natural harvest gives the birds the best possible chance of putting on weight before the first frosts, and then we might legitimately begin the artificial feeding again. But before we think of winter again, let's consider the early days of spring, and how we can encourage the birds to nest.

stock dove

rock dove

wood pigeon

collared dove

Above: *Descendants of the rock dove, most feral pigeons retain some of the plumage features of their forbears.*

Left: *Stock doves lack the white rump which most feral pigeons possess. The pure-bred rock dove is the ancestor of domesticated pigeons and their feral descendants. The wood pigeon is a wary bird in the country, but may be quite tame in a town park, and may even feed from the hand. Collared doves were unknown in Britain until the 1950s, but are familiar throughout Britain today. Equally familiar is their monotonous call.*

49

Above: *Tawny owls have become quite common in built-up areas this century. In towns they appear to take quite a lot of small birds, as well as their more usual prey of rodents.*

Right: *Introduced from the Continent in the latter half of the 19th century, the little owl's main prey consists of beetles, earthworms, moths and small rodents.*

A scarce and declining
species, the barn owl
needs all the help it can
get from anyone who
may be able to provide it
with a nest site. A
hollow tree bordering
open country, an
outhouse or ivy-clad ruin
could all be home to this
rarely seen bird. The call
is an eerie wailing. At
the nest various snoring,
hissing and bill-clicking
noises may be heard.

Above: *In some
suburban areas great
spotted woodpeckers are
regular garden birds.
They are particularly
fond of suet.*

Right: *A green
woodpecker leaves its
nest hole. Green
woodpeckers prefer more
open woodland than
their relatives, and
frequently feed on the
ground.*

Above: *The sparrow-
sized lesser spotted
woodpecker is barred
rather than spotted, and
lacks the great spotted
woodpecker's white
shoulder-patches.*

Right: *Kingfishers may
be seen perching on
lookout posts and trees
in the gardens of
waterside properties.*

Nests for all

Although we often tend to think of songbirds as nesting in trees, this is probably not the most favoured site. Most of the finches use hedges, while yellowhammers and reed buntings like bushes, often building close to the ground. Tits nest in holes, using nest boxes and holes in man-made structures as well as natural holes in trees. A treecreeper builds its nest behind a loose piece of bark, and house sparrows, house martins, swifts and swallows almost invariably use buildings. Of the regular garden nesters, only mistle thrushes and goldcrests habitually use trees, with goldfinches showing some preference for fruit trees like apples and pears. With such a choice, it should be fairly easy to provide somewhere suitable for at least one pair of birds around the house and garden.

Pruning a shrub or tree to create forks will provide nest sites for thrushes, finches and others.

TREE NESTERS

Let's consider tree nests first. All that is needed here is a fork, which occurs naturally in most trees, but which can be encouraged with judicious pruning. Trees which need to be pruned in order to encourage fruit production are ideal, because the job needs to be done anyway. Trees with thorns or prickly leaves are often chosen for the extra protection they give, so hawthorns, false acacias and hollies are all favoured trees. Evergreens, especially those with dense foliage like yews and cypresses, make excellent nest sites, and are even better when hedged, becoming practically impenetrable.

Trees that are coming to the end of their lives often develop holes where branches have broken off and, as long as they are safe, should be left to provide natural nest sites for tits, redstarts and pied flycatchers. Starlings are also tree hole nesters, so if you want to reserve your holes for the migrants you should cover them up with a close wire mesh or a stone until they return. Totally dead trees are not ideal nesting places because there are no leaves to provide cover, but woodpeckers and starlings will use them, and tits will nest in a stump quite close to the ground.

Man-made nest boxes provided with holes are, of course, the traditional way of helping birds to breed, and have been used to great effect in conifer plantations where natural holes are scarce. They are a very positive influence in the spread of the pied flycatcher, which has increased its numbers in Wales and the Lake District and spread into Yorkshire, southern Scotland, the central Highlands and the West Country. As it approaches the West Midlands conurbation from its stronghold in Wales it is becoming more frequent in gardens, where it will usually be found occupying a nest box.

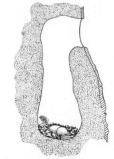

woodpecker

blackbird

Above: *Woodpeckers excavate holes in rotting tree trunks whilst blackbirds take advantage of forks in the tree for nesting.*

Below: *The same basic design is used for both hole- and open-fronted nest boxes.*

Coal, blue, great and marsh tits all use nest boxes, although willow tits prefer to excavate their own hole in the soft rotting stump of a willow, alder or birch. Nuthatches, which plaster up the entrance to a natural hole so that the entrance is just the right size for them, employ the same tactic with a nest box, even though the hole size may already be ideal! Tree sparrows are great exploiters of hole nest boxes, and owls occasionally use them, too, although they have to be purpose built.

HOUSE NESTERS

Holes in man-made structures are often exploited, and a brick or stone removed from a wall may tempt a pied wagtail or a spotted flycatcher to nest. This is a good reason for cladding buildings and walls with climbers, which screen the entrance to the nest site and afford some protection against rain and sun. Redstarts and tits sometimes use cavities in walls, as may wrens.

House sparrows, starlings and swifts tend to exploit holes under the eaves, and many people will know the frustration of being woken at first light by the scrabbling and cheeping of a brood of youngsters apparently just above their heads! The sparrows and starlings really need no encouragement to nest, but swifts can be helped by making an access slit 6.5 cm (2½ in) wide in the underside of the eaves. This should deter unwelcome guests like starlings, which usually enter the roof space through a hole in the fascia. The swifts' nests I have seen – more a scrape in the space between the rafters than a nest – weren't messy at all, so there are no health hazards, but swifts do tend to carry parasites, so if you are

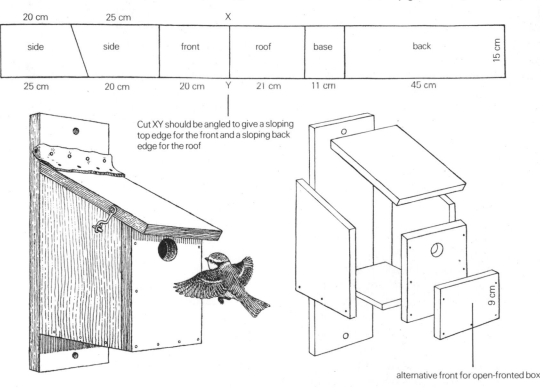

Cut XY should be angled to give a sloping top edge for the front and a sloping back edge for the roof

alternative front for open-fronted box

able to get at the nest at the end of the season you should remove any material from it to destroy anything that might survive through to the following season.

It is difficult to predict where house martins will nest, as they often ignore apparently suitable sites. They don't seem to have any particular preferences, either in terms of the house building materials or which direction the nest will face. They do like quite deep eaves which give them protection against the weather, however, and are not infrequently found nesting under the eaves at the apex of a gable. Sometimes they can be encouraged by siting an artificial house martin's nest in a suitable place, although they may choose to build their own nest next to it!

House sparrows will sometimes dispossess the martins just when they have finished building, in which case you could knock the nest down and hope that the martins will build again. (It is not an offence to destroy a house sparrow's nest, although it is illegal to do the same to house martins.) At the end of the season – about the end of October – when you can be reasonably certain that the last brood of young have left, it is a good idea to knock the empty nest down, so that the martins don't return the following year to find house sparrows have taken over. Another way of discouraging the sparrows is to hang strings 22.5 cm (8¾ in) long from the eaves, weighted with a nut, at 6 cm (2½ in) intervals. This creates too steep an angle for sparrows to fly under to enter the nest. A wooden shelf 15 cm (6 in) wide, positioned at least 30 cm (12 in) beneath the nest, will collect most of the droppings which can otherwise be a nuisance.

The house martin's close relative, the swallow, is a welcome visitor which builds its saucer-shaped mud nest in barns, sheds, garages, outside toilets, porches – in fact in any man-made structure to which it can gain

Treecreepers require rather specialized nest boxes. They are certainly worth putting up in the larger garden or one bordering woodland, however.

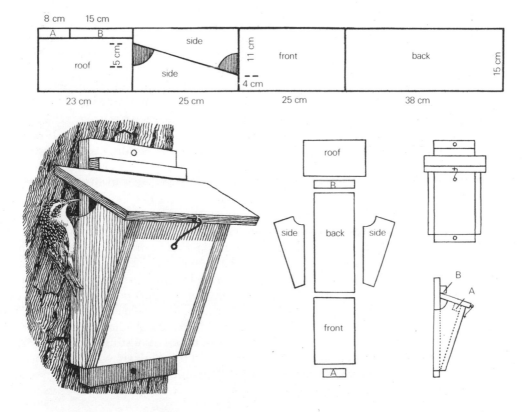

An artificial house martin nest, with a protective screen of weighted strings to discourage house sparrows.

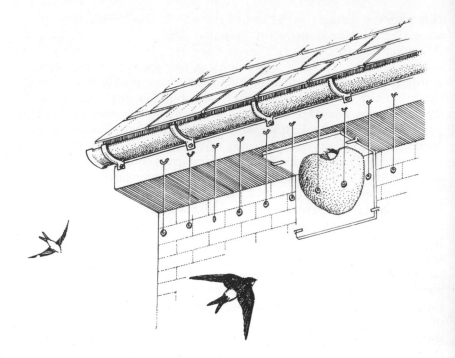

access. A door left open, a missing window pane, or a deliberately made hole in a gable end will all be taken as an invitation to enter. Robins, wrens, pied wagtails and blackbirds will also accept the invitation, building in bundles of raspberry canes, flowerpots that have fallen on their sides, on shelves, on coils of hanging wire, even in the pockets of a gardening jacket. If the invitation to nest is accepted, do ensure that you don't later close the access until nesting and fledging is complete.

Returning to holes in gables, hole nesters can be persuaded to nest if the hole is backed by a nest box. A standard open-fronted nest box fixed against the wall would be perfect. Again, if the building has some vegetation growing over it this will conceal the hole from predators and screen it against the weather. Old barns sometimes had holes in their gables so that barn owls could enter. A large shed or garage with a pitched roof might be used by owls in country districts if a nest box is also provided – either hard against the hole if the building is used, or at rafter height if there is no danger of disturbance. A tea chest, with part of it removed to form a tray, and securely fixed, would do.

Tawny owls and little owls sometimes use nest boxes which are similar to the tea chest in proportion and are sited so as to simulate the broken branch of a tree that has become hollow. Jackdaws and stock doves will also nest in this 'chimney' nest box. Jackdaws often nest in real chimneys, and not always disused ones. They block the shaft up with nest material, forming a platform for the nest itself. Despite this, young birds often fall down the chimney, so if the chimney is permanently blocked off at fireplace level it is best to do the same at the top, using a slate or roof tile.

Formerly very much cliff nesters, herring gulls have increased to such an extent this century that they have taken to nesting on roofs in seaside towns, and occasionally inland. If you particularly wanted to encourage them a platform across the roof ridge in the lee of a chimney may do the trick.

NEST BOXES

There are two standard types of nest box: one with a hole in the front, 2.8 cm (just over an inch) in diameter or less to exclude sparrows and starlings, the other with an open front. There is available from the RSPB a duel-purpose box with a drop-in front with a hole in it which converts the open-fronted box to a hole nest box. Like most other boxes sold it can be fixed on to a screw through a keyhole that is already provided in the back.

SITING A NEST BOX

It is a common mistake to site a nest box on a post, with no cover around. Birds are adept at finding concealed sites for their nests, and have perfected the art of slipping away from such a nest without being seen. Watch a bird return to its nest. It generally comes first to a nearby perch, checks the view for danger, moves to a nearer perch, checks again, and has gone to its nest in the twinkling of an eye. If the bird knows you are there and are watching it, it won't go to the nest. The second you look at something else, it has gone. Conceal yourself and watch. After a few seconds, during which you may hear the young clamouring for food, there is movement by the nest and the bird is away. If the birds that build an open nest rely on concealment for safety, hole nesters generally go for inaccessibility, using a hole on an underslope which is approached from the air. Tits like a clear view from the nest hole, so the box can be fairly exposed, but a smooth barked tree will make it more difficult for a stoat or weasel to climb to the nest. Redstarts and pied flycatchers aren't so fussy about the clear view, but don't site the box right next to a branch as you may assist a predator to reach the nest. If you are fixing a nest box to a vertical surface, incline the front towards you a little by wedging the top to prevent rain from driving in. For the same reason nest boxes should not face towards the prevailing winds, so for the British Isles the box should

A simple access slit can be made for swifts, or a more elaborate nest box complete with inspection hatch can be constructed.

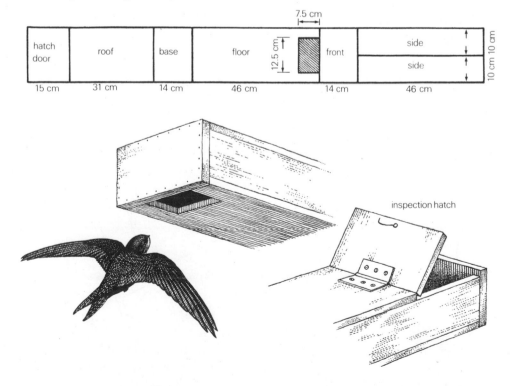

inspection hatch

face from north through east to south-east, which also prevents the midday sun from overheating the interior of the box.

Site the box in the autumn so that it has time to weather in a little and will be available as soon as nest prospecting begins in spring. It may also be used for roosting during the cold weather, and it is a delight to watch a dozen or more wrens arriving one by one to form a communal roost in a hole nest box. There is also a chance that your nest box may be tenanted by a field mouse for the winter. If you aren't able to erect the box until spring don't worry, because even if you are too late for a first brood your box may be used by birds whose first attempts have failed.

It is sometimes suggested that an open-fronted box could be sited in the fork of a tree, but if the fork is suitable it seems more sensible to leave it available for a song thrush or mistle thrush that won't use a box. If your garden is secure against mammalian predators then the height of the box is not too crucial, indeed coal tits often use natural holes that are practically at ground level. In an average garden between 1.2 and 2 m (4 and 6½ ft) is suitable, although you could go much higher on a house wall. Up to a dozen boxes to an acre (0.5 hectare) can be erected, territorial aggression seeing to it that birds likely to compete with each other will not nest too close. If you're particularly trying to encourage a migratory species to nest, block the entrance to the box until the desired species arrives.

NESTING MATERIALS

Once nest building has started, plentiful supplies of nesting material are required. If you offer material such as animal hair, straw, moss (the long sort that is used in hanging baskets) or cotton stuffed into that red mesh bag you no longer need for peanuts, you may just tip the balance in favour of nesting. Similarly, if you have a pond with natural edges you may find

Prime the inside of the owl nest box with a layer of peat. Make sure the box faces away from prevailing winds.

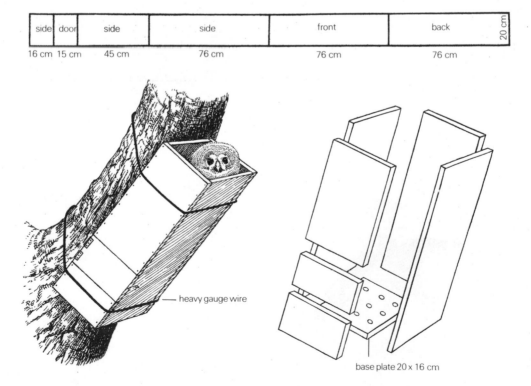

side	door	side	side	front	back	
16 cm	15 cm	45 cm	76 cm	76 cm	76 cm	20 cm

heavy gauge wire

base plate 20 x 16 cm

yourself supplying the mud lining to a thrush's nest, or the constructional material for house martins and swallows. Some moss placed in the nesting chamber of a hole nest box may prove irresistible to prospecting blue tits.

MAINTENANCE

Maintenance of nest boxes is really concerned with ensuring that they are waterproof. At the end of the season old nesting material can be removed (along with any parasites) and the interior of the box treated with a pyrethum-based insecticide. Don't use DDT, even if you still have some in the garden shed. The exterior of the box can be creosoted, as by the time the box is needed the treatment will not prove harmful to the birds. Clear polyurethane is also quite an effective waterproofing. Now is also the time to fix on a steel plate around the hole if you want to avoid the nest being raided by a squirrel or woodpecker (see the chapter on Uninvited guests). By giving the birds a chance to nest in your garden you will add immeasurably to your birdwatching pleasure. The whole range of activities that occur during the nesting period will take place before you: territorial display and song, courtship, nest-building and the rearing of young. Your bird garden will have become an all-year event.

The most highly favoured nest site is an overgrown hawthorn hedge. From this we can deduce that a whole range of songbirds appreciate the protection of the thorns, the formation of suitable forks for nesting at head height, plus the protective canopy over their heads. For this reason well-trimmed hedges are less suitable, although a properly laid hedge is the ideal foundation, and may even provide sites in its first few years. If the hedge has thorns, like blackthorn, or prickly leaves like holly, as long as the base is dense it can be allowed to become leggy. The same applies to yew, box and the hedging cypresses, where the close-clipped base will keep out predators whilst the more open top allows birds to enter and construct their nests. Dunnocks, greenfinches and goldfinches will all use the fast-growing Leyland and Lawson cypresses. Beech, hornbeam and laurel hedges make good nest sites, but beech and hornbeam need to be about 2 m (6½ ft) high and 1 m (3 ft) thick. Gorse, as a single shrub or as a hedge, is excellent and is particularly favoured by linnets and yellowhammers.

The bird garden year

Observing bird life throughout the year within a limited area can be fascinating, particularly if you keep a record of your observations. If you also record other wildlife you may be able to see how creatures interact throughout the year; over the years a discernible pattern emerges.

SPRING

As the days lengthen into March, bird social activity increases. The hurly-burly of the bird table is replaced by more subtle interactions as the birds prepare for the breeding season. Already mistle thrushes will have been singing strongly from a perch near the top of a tree and the female may be sitting on eggs. Other early nesters in gardens are robins, blackbirds and song thrushes; these species often nest two or three weeks earlier than their woodland counterparts.

Generally courtship will precede nest prospecting, but a male wren will build a number of nests, known as 'cock's nests', that he will use to court the female. Of the birds that flock in winter, many will already have formed pairs, but they still have to establish territories before they can nest successfully. By the end of March there should be plenty of bird song, some of it intended to attract a mate and some to warn other birds away from an established territory. It seems that for some resident birds song is not as important in securing a mate as it is for defending territory, as they sing most persistently in April and May when the pair is quite well established.

Outside the breeding season the male robin reacts aggressively towards the female by threat displays (right), but later, in the build up to mating, if she approaches the edge of his territory, his behaviour changes and will include courtship feeding (opposite).

Most migrants come back to the area in which they were raised, and the males start to sing as soon as they arrive in the natal area. The females usually return a few days later, by which time the males have probably spaced themselves out and are ready to receive the females. Willow warblers and chiffchaffs, the earliest migrants likely to be found in gardens, will be singing well by mid-April, and will soon have caught up with the residents in their preparations for breeding.

Whereas a blackbird may only use one song post, others will use a number to ensure that their message is communicated. Ground nesters in open places usually sing in flight, and may 'beat the bounds' of their territory. Greenfinches are the only true garden bird to sing while flying, having a distinctive 'butterfly' song flight in which they flutter and stall round the tree tops, displaying their bright underparts.

Having successfully found a mate, prospecting for a nest site begins in earnest. Blue tits will investigate nest boxes in pairs, the male entering first, reappearing at the entrance hole within seconds and then leaving to allow the female in for a look round. Tree nesters go through a similar routine, during which the female may squat in a brooding position in the potential nest site. During the period leading up to egg-laying, you may observe courtship feeding, when the female begs food from her mate, who may feed her up to seventy times a day. This strengthens the pair bond and ensures the female has all the nutrition she needs to form the eggs. It may also accustom the male to feeding the hen when she is incubating.

During this period other forms of life begin to become more noticeable, with warm days bringing out small tortoiseshell, comma and brimstone butterflies that have survived the winter in hibernation, and the first broods of the holly blue which emerges quite early during a mild spring. Holly blues are one of the few butterflies likely to have been garden-bred, as the caterpillars of many of our butterflies eat either stinging nettles or grasses. These early holly blues will have been laid as eggs on ivy the previous autumn, and spent the winter as pupae in its cover. By June this first hatch will be dead, having laid their eggs on holly, the second hatch appearing in August.

If you have a pond, now is the time to look out for the first strings of toad spawn or the sago-like mass of frog's spawn. Newts will also emerge from hibernation and make their way to water to breed. Whereas the eggs

of frogs and toads are fertilized by the male as they are laid, newts produce up to 350 eggs already fertilized, laid individually and wrapped in the leaves of water plants.

Away from the confined world of the garden pond the spring migrants are arriving, and you may get a surprise visitor, particularly if you live near the coast. Many migrants go direct to their breeding grounds, however, and it is the more leisurely return passage and the 'falls' of autumn that are likely to bring the real rarities. Nevertheless blackcaps and garden warblers may appear at this time even if they do not stay to breed, and evidence that an almost invisible migration takes place was brought home to me one spring in the form of an immaculate cock redstart that had been killed by flying into a window.

May brings the last of the migrants, the swifts and spotted flycatchers, and the breeding season is in full swing. Bird song is at its best, and if you're woken by the dawn chorus you may as well lie back and see how many songs you can recognize. Cuckoos especially will start to call very early, and this is the time of day when one may visit your garden in search of a host for its egg. Dunnocks are the commonest host in gardens, and probably second only to meadow pipits across the country. Robins and pied wagtails are also frequent victims, whereas spotted flycatchers are only occasionally parasitized.

SUMMER

By June the resident birds will be completing their first broods, and the calling of young song thrushes on the ground may attract marauding cats. Far better than moving the young bird is to frighten the cat away, because even well-fledged nestlings need vast amounts of food which their parents are much better at supplying than us. Having frightened the cat away, the best course of action is to put the young bird into cover if it is out in the open and then leave it alone. The parent birds will soon be back – if they ever really left at all – and the fledgling's calls will soon lead them to it.

June and July see a 'flush' of recently fledged birds. Most parents continue to feed the fledglings – like the pied wagtails shown below – for a few days.

Towards the end of July bird song will die out almost completely, and many birds become secretive as they go into moult. The garden pond may be heavily used for bathing if the weather is dry, and some very tatty specimens may be seen sitting on a perch near the pond, trying to rearrange their disordered feathers. This is also the time of year when

juvenile blackbirds become noticeable in their mottled plumage, causing identification problems for the inexperienced birdwatcher and creating a tingle of excitement to the keen garden lister who thinks he or she is about to add a new species to their notebook. If you live fairly close to a river or established pool your pond may be host to dragonflies, especially if you live in the south of England, although some of the daintier damselflies are found as far north as Scotland. They can be quite difficult to identify unless they are found at rest on a cool, overcast morning, but they can at least be grouped according to their style of flight – hawkers, darters, skimmers and chasers. They feed on other flying insects, often far from water and are quite harmless, but they all need water in which to breed.

In the flowerbed and shrubbery butterflies are at their best – blues, browns, peacocks and the migratory red admirals. Some of these may bear the scars of bird attack on their wings, and it has been suggested that the 'eyes' on a peacock butterfly's wing are intended to distract a would-be predator when the butterfly opens its wings to fly. If this doesn't work, then a bird will peck at the 'eye', which avoids injury to the more vital parts, such as the abdomen and thorax.

In the sky over the garden small flocks of lapwings may be seen flying off to feed on stubble or freshly ploughed fields, and black-headed gulls appear over towns to feed on flying ants and other concentrations of flying insects. Before August is out the swifts will have departed, having completed their breeding cycle in only three months. Finches begin to move about in groups, calling to each other as they fly to find fields with weeds. Greenfinches, linnets and redpolls are all recognizable by their flight calls. A charm of goldfinches may drop in to feed on cornflower seeds, and if you have sunflowers they will be descended upon by greenfinches once they begin to seed.

By mid-June lapwings are beginning to flock as they disperse away from the breeding area.

AUTUMN

As the first berries begin to ripen a return migration becomes noticeable, with bright juvenile chiffchaffs and willow warblers joining blackbirds and wood pigeons on the elderberries. Other insect-eaters such as whitethroats, lesser whitethroats and blackcaps may join them, eating as much as possible to put on maximum weight in readiness for the long flight across the English Channel, through Europe, across the Mediterranean and the Sahara until they reach their winter quarters.

In October on the coast the first winter visitors – redwings, fieldfares and bramblings – will be mingling with the last of the summer visitors like garden warblers and blackcaps, while flocks of house martins feed on the last flush of insects overhead. If you're near the sea and have rowan, elder or sea buckthorn in the garden you may be treated to this spectacle of travellers arriving and departing, replenishing lost energy or building it up. Many of the departing migrants will be juveniles, and young redstarts and pied flycatchers may turn up in any garden with shelter as they make their way towards the sea. Some late broods of house martins may still be in the nest, and if the weather changes and the flying insects disappear they may starve to death in the nest before fledging.

With the first frosts the last butterflies disappear, although a stand of Michaelmas daisies may give a small tortoiseshell butterfly enough energy to make a successful hibernation through the winter. Like the peacock and red admiral they frequently enter buildings to hibernate, finding corners in sheds and greenhouses or coming into houses to rest on the top of a window-frame behind a curtain. If you accidentally disturb one, allow it to stay indoors where its chances of survival will be high. Frogs, toads and newts will also be in hibernation by the end of October, and should be left undisturbed if discovered by chance in the garden.

WINTER

Birds are highly mobile in late autumn and early winter, many of them moving around in flocks exploiting the plentiful harvest of seeds, berries and fruits. Many finches disappear from gardens, flocking to waste ground to feed on the seeds of thistle, groundsel, dock and plantain, and moving from one patch of ground to another as they exhaust the food supply. In the evening they fly to communal roosts in evergreen shrubberies, where sparrows and greenfinches will chatter and squabble before settling down for the night.

Towards the end of day other communal roosters such as gulls, rooks, jackdaws and starlings can be seen following regular flight paths towards their chosen sites. The gulls will go to reservoirs, or if near the coast to sheltered bays, for although they feed inland extensively in winter they still seek the safety of water at night. The others go to woods, where rooks and jackdaws may roost together, although some rooks start to visit their rookeries in autumn, and may roost there. Starlings and pied wagtails may come into towns to roost, benefiting from the slightly higher temperatures experienced there. Pied wagtails seem to have a fondness for glass, packing into heated glasshouses or using the struts high above glass-covered railway stations to spend the night.

Few birds use their old nests for roosting, although house sparrows, starlings and tawny owls are among the exceptions. Treecreepers have a unique method of roosting, and you may discover a roost site by examining the main trunk of a Wellingtonia (or redwood) for the tell-tale white droppings on the bark. If you find such a site you can return after dark with a red light such as a rear bicycle lamp, (which won't wake the bird) where you will discover the treecreeper sleeping upright, pressed into a depression in the soft, fibrous bark from which it derives insulation, the feathers on the back fluffed up to trap as much air as possible to keep this part warm.

Communal roosting is thought to have a number of benefits. The most obvious is demonstrated by long-tailed tits and wrens, which huddle together for mutual warmth. It has even been shown that during the night the birds change positions, so that those on the outside have a turn on the warmer inside. There is also safety in numbers, with several hundred pairs of eyes and ears unlikely to miss a predator. If a predator does strike, however, the greater number of birds in the roost means that the odds on an individual bird becoming the victim are less. Nevertheless, sparrow-hawks and hobbies will often take advantage of roosts of wagtails, swallows and starlings, attacking the birds as they enter the roost in the evening. Tawny owls may also visit a winter roost of finches or sparrows, spreading panic among the birds and then picking one off as it flutters down to the ground in confusion. The third reason for communal roosting is that individuals benefit from group knowledge; the less experienced birds following the more experienced to a safe roost at night, then following again at dawn to find food. It is probable that this is how the scarcer visitors to the bird table, like yellowhammers and reed buntings, find their way to garden feeding stations, because they may spend the night at a roost with house sparrows, greenfinches and chaffinches which frequently visit gardens.

January, February and early March are the hardest times of the year for birds, with seeds and fruit supplies exhausted and invertebrate life locked in the soil. Despite artificial feeding and the shelter provided in gardens, inevitably some birds die. Generally, this ensures a stable population of birds, with the heavy mortality just after fledging, and the increased risk of death from cold or starvation in winter, likely to leave one adult and one young bird surviving per brood through to the next breeding season. After a particularly hard winter, however, the numbers of our smallest birds – wrens, goldcrests and long-tailed tits – may be reduced by up to 80 per cent, yet within a few years they will have regained their former numbers, the large clutch sizes and the reduced competition ensuring that more young birds make it through their first winter. From then on their rates of survival increase, although most garden birds cannot expect to live for more than two years. Remarkably, considering the immense journeys they make, the oldest individual in the summer sky of the garden is likely to be a swift, for which the oldest recorded age is twenty-one!

Cold weather may force unusual birds into the garden when a closer view may be had. Here two redwings feed on fallen fruits, with a song thrush behind.

Birdwatching

Birdwatching is all about enjoying birds, and generally in any field of activity a little knowledge adds to our enjoyment. Watching the way birds behave is easy, but sooner or later you will ask yourself, 'What is that bird?' And then, 'Why is it doing that?' So simply looking at the birds out of the window turns into something more purposeful, and you start to write things down in order to make some sense out of them, and before you know it you have a notebook and are keeping a list of the different kinds of birds you have seen in the garden. In order to identify the various species you buy an identification guide, which helps you recognize a bird when you see it without confusing you with too much detail about its natural history, and then because you can't see everything you need to make a convincing identification, you get yourself some binoculars. Really you don't need anything else, except reasonably good eyesight and hearing. Compared with many hobbies, with their subscriptions and expensive equipment, birdwatching really is good value!

It may seem premature to start offering advice about notebooks, but

Field notes of unusual species can provide valuable observations which can later be compared with a guide in order to make a positive identification.

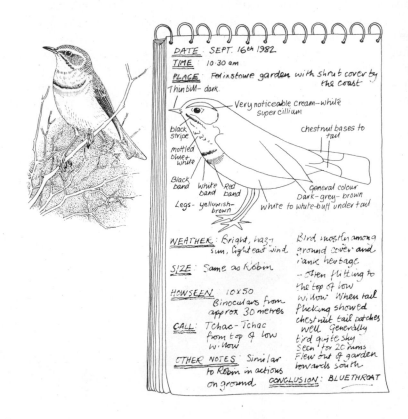

DATE: SEPT. 16th 1982
TIME: 10.30 am
PLACE: Felixstowe garden with shrub cover by the coast

Thin bill - dark.

Very noticeable cream-white super cillium

black stripe

chestnut bases to tail

mottled blue + white

Black band

White band

Red band

General colour Dark-grey- brown

white to white-buff under tail

Legs- yellowish-brown

WEATHER: Bright, hazy sun, light east wind

SIZE: Same as Robin

HOWSEEN: 10×50 Binoculars from approx 30 metres

CALL: Tchac-Tchac from top of low willow

OTHER NOTES: Similar to Robin in actions on ground

Bird mostly among ground cover and rank herbage. - often flitting to the top of low willow. When tail flicking showed chestnut tail patches well. Generally bird quite shy. Seen for 20 mins. Flew out of garden towards south.

CONCLUSION: BLUETHROAT

assuming you are going to go outside occasionally, it is worth getting a spiral-bound one, preferably with its own pencil. This means you can fold the notebook flat, so that the pages aren't flapping while you are trying to write. This book will help you identify the birds most likely to be seen in, over, or from a typical British garden, but depending in which part of the country you live, and how far from home your interest takes you, you will find yourself coming across more species than this book can cover. There are a great many bird books on the market, but for the beginner I have recommended in the bibliography several good, basic guides for the identification of both birds and other common garden wildlife.

Binoculars really need to be tried out to see what suits you, but the most suitable magnifications are 7×, 8×, and 10×. This magnification, printed on the binoculars, is always shown with another figure, for instance 7 × 50. The second number refers to the diameter of the objective lens in millimetres. The larger the objective lens, the more light that is gathered and the brighter the image you see, although as the magnification increases the image gets duller. To obtain a true picture of how bright your image will be – and this can be quite important on a dull day – divide the second figure by the first. The higher the result, the brighter the image. In any case it should not be less than 5. So 7 × 50 is brighter than 8 × 40, which is as bright as 10 × 50. If you intend using your binoculars only in the garden than a 10× magnification may be too great, because you will not be able to focus down to very short distances. Apart from that it is a matter of personal preference and cost. As a general rule, the more money you pay the better the quality of the optics, and if you choose from the range of a reputable company you will find a reliable pair of binoculars to suit your pocket. Now that you're equipped, let's do some birdwatching! What's that bird? Well, its about the size of a sparrow, but its not quite the same shape, and its not hopping and . . . we're off on the identification trail!

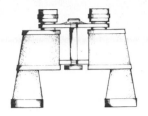

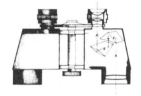

A pair of 10 × 50 binoculars (top), and a pair of 8 × 40 binoculars (above) showing how the prism arrangement reflects the light.

APPEARANCE

When people who don't know birds well try to describe one to me, they usually begin by describing its colour. But colour is very subjective, and if

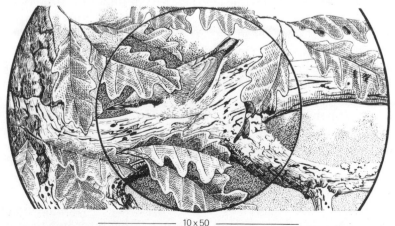

10 × 50

7 × 50

field of view of binoculars

Left: A lower magnification gives a wider field of view. For many people, a pair of 8 × 40 binoculars is the ideal compromise.

you have only a fleeting view of the bird it is often a bright wing-patch or rump that you will notice, not its main body colour. So I usually ask them to describe its size and shape, and then ask them to compare it with a bird they already know, such as a sparrow, thrush or pigeon. Other important aspects of the bird's appearance are: field marks like wing-bars, eye-stripes and rump-patches; the size and shape of the bill (for instance, short and stubby like a sparrow's, long and thin like that of a thrush, hooked like a kestrel's); whether the legs are long or short; whether the tail is long or short; and the main body colour (for instance, is it streaked or spotted, and if so on the underparts or the upperparts?).

Most of this can be described by comparison with a familiar species, and since memory is not reliable, is best written down. On a number of occasions I have not bothered to take notes, because it was too windy or cold, and then found when I got home and checked in an identification guide that I couldn't make a positive identification because I had forgotten the bill colour or some other important feature. Now if I'm in any doubt, I take notes. Although I rarely carry an identification guide – preferring to take notes while I'm watching a bird, and then comparing this later with a guide – I do usually carry a guide in the car. This is so that if I think I'm likely to see an unfamiliar species, I can check before I leave the car what field marks or behavioural characteristics I should particularly look out for.

Only by noting as much as you can about an unfamiliar bird – like this wryneck – would you be able to identify it. Behaviour may be as conclusive as appearance in some cases.

BEHAVIOUR

Unlike plants, which give you all the time in the world to identify them, birds do not keep still, rarely posing for long in that classic field guide profile. So our notes on the bird's appearance are cut short, and we find ourselves looking at the way it behaves. How does the bird fly? Strong and direct, like a starling, in little bursts, like a blue tit, or undulating, like a woodpecker? Does it soar, hover, flap its wings continuously, or does it glide? On the ground, how does it move? Some birds walk, like jackdaws, whereas a thrush will run a few paces and then stop, but may also hop. Sparrows hop, too, but dunnocks shuffle. Does the bird stay for long periods on the ground, like a starling, or keep flying up to a perch, like a robin? On the ground, starlings feed with a continuous action, bill open, probing the ground. A blackbird, by way of contrast, runs forward a few paces and then listens, head on one side, for movement in the ground below. If the bird is in a tree, how does it move then? Tits and the small finches clamber energetically among the foliage, feeding continuously. Warblers are similar, but not as acrobatic. They also sometimes progress to the top of a tree in a series of short, upward flights, interspersed with perching – a habit shared with robins and redstarts. Woodpeckers seem to bound up a tree in a series of jerks, while a treecreeper climbs in a more continuous way, in a series of rapid movements. A nuthatch, however, seems to hop vertically, going up or down with equal ease. Thrushes and jays seem to fly through trees, rocking their bodies forward when they land on a perch as if they were travelling too fast.

Some birds have special characteristics, like wing flicking, tail wagging, wing shivering and tail quivering. Other birds bob their heads. Some of the warblers have a particularly characteristic call if you

swallow

sand martin

house martin

Above: *Although superficially similar, the martins and swallows are not related to the swifts. Swallows have deeply forked tails, and generally fly lower than martins, hawking across lawns and water. They build a saucer-shaped nest in a barn or outhouse, like the one shown in the photograph on the left. Martins occupy the middle sky, between the swallows and the swifts.*

Left: *Swifts have scythe-shaped wings and little forked tails. They are all dark, flying around houses on summer evenings in 'screaming parties'. On a clear day they will fly so high that you will need binoculars to see them.*

Right: *The most regular of the crows to visit garden feeding stations, jackdaws seem to be more widely tolerated by man than the other members of their family. They often nest in close association with man, being particularly fond of buildings like churches and castles that most closely resemble their natural habitat of cliffs. Usually the nest site is a large hole or crevice, but sometimes a jackdaw will block up a chimney with sticks and make its nest there, often with disastrous consequences for the bird.*

Right: *In the country shy, woodland birds, jays are becoming increasingly common in towns and suburbs, where they are bolder and may become regular garden visitors. Although they take eggs and nestlings in spring, they are largely vegetarian in autumn and winter, and pose little threat to other birds.*

Left: *The extraordinary increase in the numbers of magpies in various parts of the country has led to the accusation that they are decimating populations of garden birds. As a rule, however, prey populations control the numbers of predators, and the super-abundance of magpies may indicate particularly high numbers of songbirds in our gardens.*

carrion crow

rook

Left: *Rooks and crows are both all-black birds, and any size difference is virtually impossible to detect in the field. The main difference is the white area at the base of bill that adult rooks possess, where there are no feathers. Immature rooks can still be told from crows when on the ground because the legs of a rook are feathered.*

Below: *Of the members of the crow family, the carrion crow is the most expert egg thief. Egg stealing is often confined to a few individuals which feed this way.*

Right: *Blue tits are always entertaining visitors to bird feeders.*

Far right: *An early nester, the long-tailed tit often starts building before most leaves are open. Here a well-camouflaged nest and the cover of gorse thorns afford some protection, however.*

Right: *A male great tit has a more prominent black breast band than his mate.*

Below: *Coal tits are very much associated with pine trees. Look for the double wing-bar and the white nape. Marsh tits generally prefer a drier habitat than willow tits.*

Coal Tit

Marsh Tit

Willow Tit

Above: *In Britain the crested tit has a restricted Scottish distribution.*

approach their nest, which takes the form of a ticking or scolding note.

SONG

Bird song is difficult to describe, and is best learned in the field. This is well worth the effort, because many birds can be identified by song alone; with chiffchaffs and willow warblers, it may be the only reliable way of separating the species. Start right at the beginning of the year, when few birds are singing, and before the migrants arrive. At first all you may hear are the silvery cadences of robins, and the occasional burst of song from a wren. You may also notice their calls, the hard 'tick' of the robin, and the scolding note of the wren. House sparrows will be cheeping, and you may hear starlings singing on mild days. Then mistle thrushes start to sing, their repetitive phrases, with long pauses, ringing out towards dusk at the end of February. Soon many of the resident birds will be joining in, and because the leaves aren't open yet you should be able to see them as they sing, and identify them. By the time the first migrants arrive you should be familiar with about a dozen songs, depending where you live, and should be able to cope with a few more. By restricting yourself to the garden, and perhaps a local park or wood, you shouldn't become overwhelmed, and increasing familiarity will make you more confident in your identification.

A starling sings from a typical perch – a roof top.

There are various clues to help you link a song to a particular bird. A blackbird will sing from an exposed perch, with its head held up. Starlings may look similar, singing from a television aerial, but they often flutter their wings while they sing. Collared doves sing their monotonous song out in the open, too, whereas a turtle dove croons from deep cover, often quite low down. Blackcaps and garden warblers tend to babble from the middle of rhododendrons; whitethroats from the edge of a hawthorn, sometimes briefly flying up and singing at the same time, before dropping back into the bush. Willow warblers and chiffchaffs often sing from trees with open foliage, like birches and willows, sometimes quite high up, but usually towards the end of a branch. Some songs are made up of repeated phrases, but even a nightingale's song can be broken up into a number of phrases to help you remember it.

The chiffchaff's song, from which it takes its name, is really unmistakeable once you've noticed it. Similarly the cuckoo's, although some people mistake a collared dove's three-syllable song for a cuckoo's until they really do hear a cuckoo. The hoot of an owl, the screech of a swift, and the cawing of a rook are other easily recognized and memorized 'songs'. Calls are often parts of a song, like the tinkling call of a goldfinch in flight, and are mainly used by flocking birds to maintain contact. Finches often call in flight, while tits usually call as they move through trees in mixed groups in autumn and winter. The great tit calls in flight, in trees, at any time of the year, and has a bewildering variety of notes. Some are almost songs, others just one note repeated. Having familiarized myself with the usual repertoire, I now reckon to learn at least one new one each year. Fortunately great tits are unique in having so many calls, and generally they are an aid to identification, not a hindrance. The easiest way of learning calls is to be out birdwatching with someone who knows them well because, unlike song, which usually gives you time to locate the bird

A chaffinch flying away, showing distinctive patterns of black and white. Combined with a knowledge of the bird's habits, this will be enough to make a positive identification.

visually to complete identification, calls may be infrequent and produced by a moving bird.

HABITAT

The last ingredient in successful bird recognition is knowing what birds to expect in any given habitat, and at what time of the year they are likely to be encountered. This has become much easier in the last decade, because our knowledge of the distribution of breeding birds has been enhanced by a number of publications based on extensive field work, culminating in the 'Atlas': *The Atlas of Breeding Birds in Britain and Ireland*.

Field studies, undertaken by volunteers working under the direction of the British Trust for Ornithology (BTO) have recently been completed on the status of our birds in winter, so soon we will have a very accurate picture of bird distribution outside of the main migration periods. Consequently most identification guides now have accurate (although necessarily generalized) distribution maps for all our resident and regular migratory birds, which is a vast improvement on the rather vague statements that used to indicate a bird's range, and so often led to faulty identification. The only way to learn about bird distribution is to read about it, but while you are still learning it is essential to check this when comparing your notes with an identification guide description.

JIZZ

When experienced birdwatchers describe a bird to each other, they may talk about its 'jizz'. What they are referring to is the bird's character, as well as the combination of appearance and behaviour. It embraces some of the things about a bird's appearance that are difficult to describe, like the 'gentle' appearance of a common gull when compared with a black-headed gull, or the 'angry' look of a fieldfare. 'Jizz' can be very important when you are confronted with an unfamiliar bird. It is the 'jizz' of the juvenile blackbird that tells the birdwatcher that this is indeed a blackbird

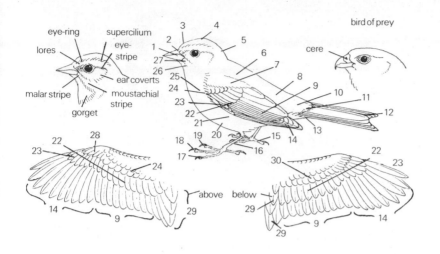

Left: *Get to know the names of the parts of a bird.*
1 *lower mandible*
2 *upper mandible*
3 *forehead*
4 *crown*
5 *nape*
6 *mantle*
7 *scapulars*
8 *back*
9 *secondaries*
10 *rump*
11 *upper tail coverts*
12 *tail feathers*
13 *under tail coverts*
14 *primaries*
15 *hind toe*
16 *tarsus*
17 *outer toe*
18 *middle toe*
19 *inner toe*
20 *belly*
21 *flank*
22 *secondary wing coverts*
23 *upper primary coverts*
24 *lesser wing coverts*
25 *breast*
26 *throat*
27 *chin*
28 *bastard wing*
29 *axillaries*
30 *wing lining*

0 (calm)
1 (light breeze)
2 (light breeze)
3 (gentle breeze)
4 (moderate breeze)
5 (fresh breeze)
6 (strong breeze)
7 (moderate gale)
8 (gale)
9 (strong gale)
10 (whole gale)
11 (storm)
12 (hurricane)

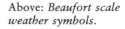

Above: *Beaufort scale weather symbols.*

in an unfamiliar plumage, and not a rare thrush from Asia! It is 'jizz' which tells us that a fleeting shape is a spotted flycatcher, or that the silhouette on a bush by the road is a corn bunting and not a house sparrow. By getting to know the birds in your garden, and absorbing their 'jizz', you will find bird recognition in new surroundings much easier, because you will have a reliable basis for comparison.

FIELD NOTES

Once you have become used to looking at and listening to birds in the way described, you will need to make notes of them in a way that you and others can easily understand. In describing a bird's appearance, you really need to know the names of the parts of a bird in order to describe it accurately. And simply knowing that you can describe eight different parts to a bird's wing will help to focus your attention to detail. A field sketch, no matter how clumsy, is always a useful way of showing field marks.

Time of day and date are also essential, and also standard abbreviations for weather details and wind speeds. Because I tend to forget these, I have stuck a copy of these in my notebook for reference, and you could do the same with a plumage diagram. There are no standard abbreviations for describing habitat, but for most situations descriptions like 'arable farmland' will do. If, however, you are puzzled over an identification, or think you're on to a rarity, then a fuller description should be noted, for instance, 'arable farmland, no hedges but line of pollard willows along stream marking field edge; field was cabbages, adjoining fields of barley'. If you wanted to add any extra detail, a sketch map would be useful.

LOOKING AT BIRD BEHAVIOUR

With identification becoming a more natural part of your birdwatching, let's look at some aspects of bird behaviour unconnected with naming the birds. If the bird garden has been laid out with regard to sight lines, you

should be able to watch most of the activities of the birds as they go about their daily lives. In many ways watching from an upstairs window is more fun, because it gives you a wider field of view, so that you may be able to anticipate incidents before they occur.

Imagine there is a blackbird feeding on your lawn in mid April. It is likely that he considers your lawn as part of his territory, especially as he sings regularly from the top of one of your trees. How is he going to react to the male blackbird you can see flying towards the garden? The new bird lands on your fence, cocking its tail up as it lands in characteristic fashion. Is this some sort of signal? The first bird is too occupied with a worm to notice the intruder. The second bird leaves its perch, alights on the lawn and runs forward a few paces before stopping, again cocking its tail. Now your bird has noticed. It runs forward, a worm in its bill, and begins to chase the newcomer, which takes flight out of your garden and across your neighbour's before landing on their shed roof. Your bird stops on the fence, in almost exactly the same spot as the intruder was perched, and scolds loudly, wings raised, tail cocked. The other bird replies, scolding just as loudly, but neither advances.

After a few seconds your blackbird flies back on to the lawn, runs a few steps and then flies to the post at the end of the clothes line. He looks round, and then flies directly into the hawthorn hedge on the far side of the garden. You didn't notice if he was still carrying the worm, but suspect that he was going to feed an incubating mate. If you keep watching you should see him leave the hedge, and can follow his movements to see if there is a nest. The whole incident has taken about thirty seconds, but it has told you a lot about how and why these blackbirds are interacting, and left some unanswered questions, too. Why do blackbirds cock their tails in that particular way? Do any other birds do a similar thing? Is it the same sort of behaviour as a pied wagtail's wagging tail?

The truth is that the science of ornithology still has much to learn about bird behaviour, because although much has been recorded, it is often difficult to interpret. Much of what has been noted about bird behaviour has been done by enthusiastic amateurs, often under the guidance of the British Trust for Ornithology, which has a small professional staff who instigate enquiries, co-ordinate the effort, and collate the information gathered. Nearly all we know about the populations of common birds, the birds that visit gardens and the food they prefer, has come from information gathered by volunteers, and can be used for the benefit of birds. So if you enjoy observing and recording you can make a very real contribution to the welfare of birds at the same time.

PREENING

There are so many aspects of bird behaviour to watch that you could almost keep a notebook of one activity alone. Take preening for example. After feeding, this is the most important activity that a bird undertakes, because if the feathers aren't cared for the bird will be unable to fly, will become cold and wet, riddled with parasites and easy meat for a predator, and will not even be able to function on a social level by displaying. So feather care occupies a lot of the time not spent feeding, and involves a whole range of activities. Let's return to our blackbird. Taking the country as a whole, blackbirds are probably the most numerous garden bird. They are not timid, approaching houses quite close, and live most of their lives in a fairly small area, so if we have one in the garden we are not likely to miss any of its usual behaviour.

The most obvious form of feather care is preening, which takes place at any time of the day, but is always most scrupulous after bathing. Does our blackbird bathe at any particular time of the day? Is bathing undertaken the same number of times each day? Does the weather have any effect on either? Although you may not be able to watch the garden all day, you can certainly log when you do notice bathing, and with your usual note of weather and time of day this may soon build into a pattern.

Now watch your blackbird bathe. He gets low down in the water, feathers raised, dips his head and flicks water on to his back, which is then spread as the wings flap. All this takes place as a few rapid movements, with occasional pauses sometimes to nibble at the breast feathers. How long is the bathing period? Does weather seem to affect the length of time the bird stays in the water? Is drinking associated with bathing or is it quite a separate activity? Then the blackbird leaves the water with a few hops and flies directly to a perch about 2 m (6½ ft) away – the same branch it used yesterday. Now preening begins in earnest. The bird shakes itself vigorously, fluffing up the feathers, and nibbling its breast again. Then it turns its head and nibbles at the base of its tail, then starts to work at the wing coverts. In fact our blackbird is stimulating its preen gland to secrete oil which is then smeared over the feathers. Soon you can see the preen gland quite easily, like a bald patch. The first time I noticed this I thought the bird was suffering from some sort of canker! The oil appears to work as a kind of conditioner, but not all birds have a preen gland, so it would be interesting to know what they use as a substitute.

A jay anting. About forty passerine species have been recorded displaying this behaviour.

How often does the blackbird get oil on its bill, and does it seem to preen its feathers in any particular sort of order? How long does this part of preening take? Having nibbled, run its bill down the entire length of its flight feathers, and scratched its head with its foot, the blackbird wipes its bill vigorously on its perch from side to side, suddenly sits upright and flies off. Was it disturbed?

And so you could go on, recording every facet of this one bird's behaviour; including sunbathing or anting, that strange behaviour whereby the blackbird half-squats among some ants, its wings outstretched, and allows them to run all over itself. Over twenty British species have been seen anting, jays being the most frequently observed. It seems that birds do this in order to control mites, which are killed by the release of formic acid from the ants (their 'sting'). Those that aren't killed quickly run at random, making it much easier for the host to remove them than when they are hidden among the barbs of the feathers. After anting, the bird usually bathes. Other feather care techniques recorded are dust-bathing and powdering, which replaces oiling in some pigeons. But there may be other activities associated with preening which have yet to be noted.

DISPLAY

Another facet of bird behaviour that will repay study is display. This has two forms, aggressive and sexual, and most of the time there is not a great deal of difference between them. This may come as no surprise to those of us who have watched adolescents of both sexes 'larking about'. A set of signals between male and female that are a prelude to mating become the means by which one male establishes dominance over another. Birds like robins, where the sexes look the same, will initially react much as if they were the same sex. When a female robin enters the territory of a male towards the end of winter, she will be greeted with an aggressive display. She may flee temporarily, but attracted by the male's song she will soon return. This time she reacts to the males' aggression by crouching in a submissive display, which inhibits the male's tendency to aggression. She will probably remain on the edge of his territory for a few days, always submitting to his displays, until gradually she is accepted. Then the display turns to courtship, and soon the female, with wings quivering,

House sparrows frequently court in groups, the cocks puffing out their chests and hopping round the hen with their wings drooped.

coal tit

great tit

blue tit

will be fed by the male, and eventually mating takes place.

House sparrows are noisy and conspicuous birds, and it is quite easy to watch their social behaviour without disturbing them. They often display in groups, a single male displaying to a female soon being joined by other males, attracted by the chirping. Soon they are all puffing out their breasts, drooping their wings and bowing, until the female decides she has had enough and flees, pursued by the whole flock. Sometimes violent tussles occur, but generally encounters are restricted to posturing and threats, and injuries are rare.

Bird tables force birds to feed unnaturally close to each other, and aggressive displays are common. If your table is near to a window, or you have a feeder hanging there, it is usually possible to distinguish between individuals of the same species. Then you can not only observe dominance between the species, but also between individuals. Among tits the great tit is unsurprisingly the most dominant, then comes the blue tit, which is smaller than the less dominant marsh tit, and finally the coal tit, which is the smallest of the group. Willow tits and long-tailed tits are not sufficiently regular visitors to feeders for us to see a pattern emerging, but my guess is that the diminutive long-tailed tit would dominate the larger, but timid willow tit, and possibly the coal tit, too. With half a dozen or so birds on one feeder in cold weather, it is interesting to see how close to one another the tits will feed. When one approaches too close, the dominant bird raises its wings, hissing at or scolding the submissive bird at the same time. Usually the less dominant bird flutters off, returning to the other side of the hanging feeder, but sometimes it only has to move a few millimetres for the aggressive display to stop.

ABOVE THE GARDEN

Because my garden is not yet fully established, and has no large trees, I have a very good view of the sky. Because of this I tend to regard birds seen over, or from the garden, as part of the garden avifauna, but I am curious about their activities further afield. For instance, in July I have noticed large numbers of rooks and jackdaws travelling high in a north-easterly direction, in early afternoon. This is the same way they go to roost in winter, and indeed I have also seen them doing this in early evening in July. It seems unlikely that they will go to roost so early, so why and where are they going? Alternatively, it may be more relevant to ask where they have come from. There is a refuse dump just over a kilometre from my home, and crows, rooks and jackdaws are all common there or on the adjacent fields. It seems probable that the birds have been disturbed by earth-moving machinery, and are going elsewhere to feed, in the general direction of the roost. Similar phenomena that you may see from your garden are V-formations of gulls going to roost, or flights of starlings. Of course it is not practical to go chasing across country after birds to see where they are heading, but there is another method if your curiosity is aroused.

Take the gulls, for instance. If you live in an inland town, they are almost certainly heading for a nearby lake. Using a ruler and a map, you can work out their most probable destination, simply by laying the ruler on the map in the general direction that the birds are flying, and finding the nearest area of water on that route. To confirm your theory, choose a spell of settled weather and check the time that the gulls pass overhead on two or three consecutive days. Then make a rough calculation of how long it may take the gulls to reach their destination – they will be flying at something like 40 kph (25 mph) unless there are strong winds – and what time they should arrive there. Having checked in advance that you will get reasonable views at the predicted roost site, go there yourself, making sure you arrive well before the gulls, and wait to see if a similar number of gulls of the same species arrive on schedule. If they arrive on time but their numbers have doubled, don't be dismayed. Other groups of gulls will doubtless be converging on the same place and may have joined up with 'your' group. You could try the same technique with rooks or starlings, when you may be rewarded with the sight of a sparrowhawk that has come to prey on the roost.

Towards the end of October, parties of migrating fieldfares pass over my garden, heading west. Invariably I hear them before I see them, their 'chack-chack-chack' calls alerting me to look up. Usually there are only a dozen or so, but occasionally groups of about forty have passed over. Counting birds in flight can be difficult, even when they are flying in formation, unless you simplify the matter. The easiest method is to sub-divide the group of birds, counting the first ten and then estimating the groups of ten after that. I once counted 120 starlings on a short stretch of telegraph wire by this method and didn't believe the result. I checked it by counting individual birds, and was only 3 out. With very large numbers of birds, like a flock of waders on an estuary, the trick is to reach ten groups of ten, and then count in groups of a hundred, or even a thousand.

Not long after I've noticed the fieldfares, it is the turn of redwings. These attractive thrushes make their sea crossings by day, but make further stages of their migration at night, when you may hear their thin 'tseep' contact calls as the birds pass overhead. Later on in the winter, prolonged snow or freezing conditions may force the redwings on a further migration, when they will tend to head south or west. These migrations are called cold weather movements, and are also undertaken by fieldfares and skylarks, both recognizable by their contact calls, and lapwings, which are quite easily recognized by their 'floppy' black-and-white wings. If much of the West Country is also frozen they will make their way to Ireland, France or even Portugal in the search for milder weather. If conditions change, and the weather improves quite quickly, the birds make return migrations, and can be seen generally heading east.

Whenever I hear the alarm calls of starlings or house martins, I look up.

A treecreeper finds a warm roosting place in the soft bark of a redwood tree.

Usually the reason is a kestrel, for a pair generally nest nearby. Although kestrels are capable of taking a young martin in flight they will be mobbed, the kestrel lazily circling round surrounded by a twittering mob, until it has had enough and goes into a long glide away from its tormentors. Once the cause of the alarm was a hobby, but this bird, also a juvenile, seemed disinterested in the house martins that surrounded it, eventually catching a flying insect in its claws, which it then passed up to its bill to eat in flight. Recent research conducted by the RSPB has shown that hobbies are not as scarce as is generally supposed, and it is certainly worth looking hard at any kestrel on the off-chance that it may be a hobby. In the west of Britain buzzards are seen over gardens quite regularly, and skeins of geese may be seen in areas where they are numerous in winter. Other large birds, easily recognized in flight, that are frequently seen from gardens are herons, mute swans (and no doubt also the occasional Bewick's or whooper), Canada geese and shelducks. Near the coast and certain inland lakes and reservoirs cormorants can quite often be seen labouring over, as they travel from one favoured spot to another.

THE BTO NEST RECORD SCHEME

If you have birds nesting in the garden, you may like to join the BTO's Nest Record Scheme. This enquiry, started in 1939, now receives upwards of 20,000 completed cards a year, the continuity of some of the garden data being particularly valuable in showing long-term trends. A record card is issued to anyone who is prepared to complete it, and has full instructions on the reverse.

The front of the card, apart from recording the observer's name, address and site details, gives space for a description of the nest and its site, and the whole nesting sequence from nest building through to fledging. If the nest is deserted or the eggs raided by a predator during this time the record is still valid, as it completes a picture of nesting attempts, giving the analyst information on success and failure.

Great care must be taken during the observation period not to disturb

A brood of recently fledged swallows lines up for feeding time.

the birds in any way, but a great deal of information can be gathered from watching from a distance and a few nest inspections. During nest building, when the birds are especially wary, much can be learned from watching the birds carry nest material. Coarse items like twigs and grass suggest that building is in its early stages, finer material like feathers and moss indicate that the nest is being lined. When nest-building appears to have ceased, a visit to the nest to establish when egg laying has started will be necessary. As most garden birds lay only one egg a day, usually in the morning, and don't start to incubate until the clutch is complete, it should be safe to inspect the nest in the afternoon, when the female should be away feeding.

Once it has been established that egg laying has commenced, an interval of a week can be allowed while the clutch is completed. If you are recording the nest of one of the tits, this inspection can be delayed even longer, as it is probable that more than ten eggs will be laid. When you do make your next inspection, try to establish when the incubating bird has left the nest to feed, checking the clutch size as quickly as possible, but taking great care not to disturb the surrounding vegetation. Most songbirds need a fortnight to hatch their eggs, so you need visit the nest no more than three or four times before you should be able to establish the date of hatching. Some three to four days after the first eggs hatch it should be possible to count the completed clutch and a week later you can count the young. After this it is better to try and establish how many young reach the fledgling stage by waiting for them to leave the nest, as a premature inspection can cause the young birds to 'explode', or burst from the nest. This is a safety device intended to protect the young if a predator attempts to rob the nest at this stage; the shock administered to the predator should give the young time to hide. Although leaving the nest early is risky, it is safer than facing a nest predator. Families of tits and swallows can be particularly obliging at this stage, lining up along a branch close to the nest to be fed. Thrushes, blackbirds and robins tend to disperse quite quickly, hiding under shrubs or sitting in the middle of a bush, calling to the parent to be fed. Swallows and house martins may come back to the nest to roost for a few days, but the young from an open-topped nest will spend the night nearby in a hedge.

If for any reason the nest fails, keep following the fortunes of the pair, as they will certainly build again. Even when nesting has been abandoned because of the death of one bird, a new mate may be found in days, because there will always be a floating population of unmated birds. This may be due to a lack of suitable nest sites, a lack of suitable territory due to

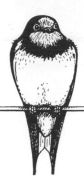

a high population of the species in question, or the birds' immaturity.

Many garden birds rear two or more broods per season, relining the old nest and recommencing egg laying within a week to a fortnight. If the nesting attempt follows a failure then egg laying may start as soon as four days after the previous attempt was abandoned. Completed cards relating to the same pair of birds should be clipped together, otherwise a misleading pattern could emerge.

THE COMMON BIRDS CENSUS

Away from the garden, the BTO runs a similar scheme aimed at recording the populations of common birds in farmland and woodland. The purpose of the exercise is similar to the Nest Record Scheme, the collected data being analysed to show population trends, research being initiated if the results seem to indicate dramatic short-term, or steady long-term changes in the numbers of our common birds.

About three hundred observers take part, covering the same area each year so that after a time a pattern emerges. The first farmland CBC took place in 1963, following probably the harshest winter nationwide for over two hundred years. Low populations of wrens and song thrushes and other vulnerable species were recorded, and consequently 1966 was chosen as the year against which population trends should be gauged. By this time woodland areas were also being censused, and the CBC has been able to follow the fortunes of a number of species going through population dynamics.

The wren population, down to 20 per cent of its level in the year preceding the disasterous winter of 1962/3, took five breeding seasons to recover to the pre-1962 level. In woodland it stabilized, but showed continued growth in farmland for the next two years, suggesting that the woodland habitat was now saturated and the birds were being forced to colonize more marginal habitats. The CBC has also shown the continuing decline of the song thrush compared with the dynamic blackbird, a trend which appears to have started during the cold winters of the forties, which the harsh weather of 1962/3, 1978/9 and 1981/2 has confirmed. The cause seems to be in the song thrush's diet, depending much more heavily on earthworms and other ground-dwelling invertebrates than its close relative.

In 1969 the CBC revealed a 60 per cent or more drop in the numbers of whitethroats returning to breed that year, continuing drought in its wintering areas being thought to be the cause of high winter mortality. A similar fate seems to have befallen the sand martin.

The census method used in the CBC is not as detailed as the nest record scheme, being aimed at establishing the numbers of breeding pairs of a species by mapping the territories of the breeding males. The song posts of the singing male are recorded over a number of visits, and when mapped will show up as clusters which indicate an established territory. Males not holding territory will show up in isolation after successive visits, and are not counted in the final total. When the census period is over, the various species can be mapped separately, and the number of territories for a species within the census area are clearly shown.

Like the nest record scheme, the value of the CBC lies in its ability to monitor population changes, enabling conservationists to act positively for the welfare of the birds with the support of hard facts behind them.

PHOTOGRAPHY

You may find that having attracted birds into the garden, rather than just watching them and perhaps recording their activities in a notebook, you want to record them on film. However, unlike birdwatching which is relatively inexpensive, for bird photography you will find that you will need to invest in some costly equipment in order to get results even approaching those of the professionals, unless you are already a keen amateur photographer. And if patience and stealth are required for birdwatching, this is doubly true for the bird photographer.

The equipment you need will depend to some extent on what standard you wish to attain, but unless you have very tame birds you will certainly need a telephoto lens. These can range from 100 mm to 1000 mm, the price increasing with the focal length. A 35 mm camera body is the most

Camera and flash unit set up on a favoured spot. With plenty of lead, the flash could be placed nearer the subject.

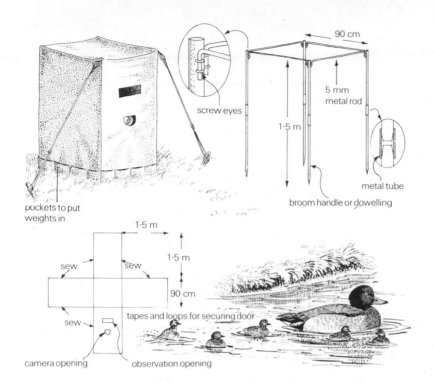

screw eyes

90 cm

5 mm
metal rod

1·5 m

metal tube

broom handle or dowelling

pockets to put
weights in

1·5 m

1·5 m

sew

sew

90 cm

sew

tapes and loops for securing door

camera opening

observation opening

*An easily demountable
hide set up by a pond,
river landing stage or
feeding station will help
you get closer to your
subject.*

versatile type, and should have through-the-lens light metering and focus-ing, with the facility to change lenses. As with binoculars, any reputable make will be capable of good results, but you will only get what you pay for. I don't think there is any consensus among bird photographers about which camera to use, but the one thing they will all agree on is that a good quality lens is paramount. The reasons are fairly straightforward. In order to bring your image closer to you, you need a lens with a long focal length, which cuts down the amount of light reaching the film. This means you have to compensate by using a slow shutter speed or a wider aperture to your lens, which increases the amount of light. To try and overcome these problems, most wildlife photographers use high-speed flash to create extra light, thereby enabling them to use a smaller aperture and hence give them a greater depth of field (region of sharp focus).

So how do you go about setting things up so that you get a photograph without frightening the bird? First and foremost consider the welfare of the bird, and for this reason nest photography should be avoided. Nest photography probably flourished in the early days because it was the only way that the photographer could guarantee the presence and co-operation of the bird for long enough to get the photograph, thereafter becoming the accepted way of approaching the subject. With more sophisticated equipment being available, and with many bird photographers more keen to obtain a shot of the bird away from the nest, this is no longer necessary or desirable.

Two sites in the garden are ideal for photography, the pond and the feeder. For a more natural look many photographers bait a branch or log with peanuts, fat or mealworms, which can be pushed into a crevice and need not show on the picture. Having decided on your sites and camera position, you can now choose your style of photography: hide or remote

Creating the effect of running water encourages birds to investigate. Warblers seem to be particularly attracted to 'running' water. The arrangement shown here can be set up easily to achieve the desired effect, providing you with some interesting subjects for photography.

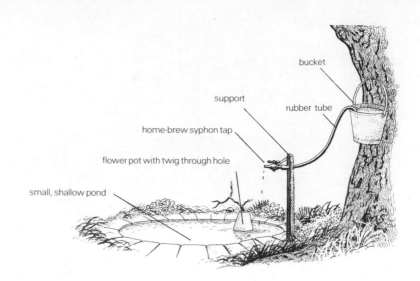

bucket

support

rubber tube

home-brew syphon tap

flower pot with twig through hole

small, shallow pond

control. Most people will be familiar with the function of a hide, and a portable one can be bought relatively cheaply, or made at home. In order to fool any birds that may be watching, you will need someone to accompany you to the hide, who should then leave when you have entered. Birds, it seems, cannot count, and seeing one person leave the hide are satisfied that there is no danger. Once inside the hide, you will need to sit still in very cramped conditions, until your subject appears. If you hand hold the camera you will be able to react to any situation that may arise, although your pictures may suffer from camera shake. With a tripod there is no risk of this, but you may find that by the time you've repositioned the camera your bird has flown.

An alternative method is to use remote control. This avoids the long periods of inactivity in the hide and substitutes them with equally long periods of near motionlessness by a window. You will need to have your camera set up and pre-focused on a favoured drinking or bathing place, or the baited log, and will need a long remote control lead and automatic wind-on. Having set everything up, you now wait in the comfort of your home and simply press the shutter release at the appropriate moment. The skill is in the initial setting up, based on your knowledge of the behaviour of the birds that visit your garden. The disadvantage of this method is that you cannot of course make adjustments if your subject doesn't pose quite where you would have liked or if lighting conditions change dramatically. Simpler than all these methods is to crouch by an open window, resting the camera on the window sill, and take your shots from there. Remember to wear a mask and gloves to avoid alarming the birds with your face and hands.

Birds of the garden

In this identification section various generalizations have been made to give an indication of the size of birds. Where practical a comparison with a familiar species has been made; elsewhere the usual adjectives are used. The terms of comparison used relate like this: **very small** – goldcrest, wren; **small** – tits, redpoll, siskin, treecreeper; **sparrow sized** – quite small; **starling sized** – not large; **thrush sized** – not small; **blackbird sized** – quite large; **pigeon sized** – large; **very large** – heron, swan. On the illustrations, where symbols are used ♂ denotes male and ♀ denotes female.

Grey heron *Ardea cinerea*
☐ **Status** Resident. Widely distributed across the British Isles. May move to the coast in winter.
☐ **Habitat** Rivers, streams, lakes, reservoirs, marshes and estuaries.
☐ **Identification** Very large; may stand hunched with neck sunk down or neck elongated; sinuous. Grey back; white head, neck and underparts; crown black and crested; neck marked with black chevrons. Juvenile lacks crest; has grey crown and neck. Dagger-shaped bill and long yellow legs. Length 90 cm (36 in).
☐ **Behaviour** Stands motionless at water's edge or wades gracefully in margins. Catches fishes, frogs, rats and voles by seizing prey in bill, not by impaling. Prey swallowed whole (fishes head-first). Flight steady; wing-beats slow, with trailing legs and neck withdrawn. Acrobatic when evading mobbing crows, etc.
☐ **Voice** A harsh 'frank'; noisy at nest site.
☐ **Nesting** Breeds colonially in tops of trees, occasionally on ground in reeds. Nest bulky, constructed of twigs. Lays February to May; one brood, three to five light blue eggs; incubation about twenty-five days, by both sexes. Young leave after seven or eight weeks.
☐ **General notes** Familiar as a raider of ornamental ponds, although it may be seen flying over if garden is near water. Sometimes circles to gain height, then glides down to next hunting place. Has special claw for grooming off slime from fishes. Known to visit bird tables in hard weather.

Mallard *Anas platyrhynchos*
☐ **Status** Resident. Widely distributed throughout the British Isles. Numbers increased in winter by Continental birds.
☐ **Habitat** Water of all kinds, but rarely on the sea.
☐ **Identification** Large. Drake (male) has glossy green head, grey body,

chestnut breast with white neck-ring; distinctive purple-blue wing-patch (speculum) and upturned tail feathers; bill yellow. Female is mottled yellowish-brown; orange colour on bill; speculum as male. Dark hybrids often occur. Drake in eclipse (July to September) resembles female. Length 58 cm (23 in).

☐ **Behaviour** Swims fairly low in water; waddles on land. Feeds by dabbling at water's edge, up-ending, or grazing. All kinds of animal and vegetable matter eaten, sometimes coming to stubble to feed on spilt grain. Flight is fast and direct; launches almost vertically into air from water surface, skids on landing. May spend long periods loafing on river bank or landing pier. On rivers often tame, elsewhere can be wary.

☐ **Voice** The classic 'quack', but uttered by female only. Male has quieter nasal call. Young 'peep' continually when following parent.

☐ **Nesting** Often at considerable distance from water, especially in towns. Nest is leaves and grass – lined with down – in undergrowth, tree hole, or hollow in the ground. Will nest in woven duck basket placed on island, raft or in undergrowth near water. Lays February to May; one brood; seven to sixteen pale green or olive eggs; incubation about twenty-eight days, by female only. Young leave nest almost straight away, flying at about six weeks.

☐ **General notes** Our most common duck; ancestor of farmyard ducks. May visit riverside gardens to loaf or graze on lawn, attracted by grain or bread. Sexes look the same during 'eclipse', when flight feathers are moulted and camouflage is then an advantage to the male.

Sparrowhawk *Accipiter nisus*

☐ **Status** Resident. Now regaining lost ground from population crash in 1960s due to pesticide poisoning. Still uncommon in parts of eastern England. Continental birds swell resident population in winter.

☐ **Habitat** Woodland, and farmland with copses and hedgerows. Edges of moorland or marsh in winter.

☐ **Identification** Pigeon sized, but with short, rounded wings and a long tail. Male has blue-grey upperparts and barred chestnut-and-white underparts. Female is larger; grey-brown above, barred grey-brown below. Immature is like browner female. Yellow legs and eyes noticeable at close range. Length 30–38 cm (12–15 in).

☐ **Behaviour** Hunts by surprise. Feeds on small birds by cruising along one side of a hedge then flipping over to the other side or appearing suddenly round the corner of a wood. Also soars like a miniature buzzard. In direct flight has flap-flap-glide sequence.

☐ **Voice** Harsh, chattering 'kek-kek-kek'.

☐ **Nesting** Builds a twig nest in a tree, often a larch, in a copse or wood; nest often decorated with green material. Lays in May; one brood; four to six white eggs, blotched red-brown; incubation about thirty-five days, by female only. Young leave twenty-four to thirty days after hatching.

☐ **General notes** Increasingly seen from gardens in north and west. May enter gardens (even, rarely, a house) in pursuit of prey. Otherwise may visit feeding station to catch small birds. Usually seen in flight; doesn't hover. Incubation starts as soon as first egg is laid, so young develop at different stages. If food shortages occur, youngest birds die first, enabling the older nestlings to survive.

Left: *The nuthatch gets its name from its method of opening nuts, particularly hazels, which are wedged in a crevice in the bark of a tree and hammered open with powerful blows of the dagger-shaped bill. Nuthatches move with equal ease both up, and down, a tree trunk as they search for food.*

Left: *A rusty-brown ball of feathers darting into cover is all many people see of a wren, which is possibly why they are generally regarded as uncommon. In fact, they are our most widely distributed bird.*

Below: *Treecreepers are superbly camouflaged, often revealing themselves only by their high, thin calls. Their characteristic behaviour is to spiral up the main trunk of a tree in a series of jerks, eventually flying down to the base of a nearby tree to start all over again. A typical nest site is behind a loose flap of bark, especially on a redwood tree.*

Right: *A mistle thrush sings from a typical perch – high up in a tree among the unopened buds.*

Far right: *A female blackbird tends her brood. This is a typical garden nest site.*

Below: *Newly arrived fieldfares strip a rowan of its berries. When all the berries have been eaten, fieldfares will be found on meadows and playing-fields.*

redstart

redwing

juvenile

Below: *The redstart gets its name from its red tail, which is continuously flicked.*

Bottom: *For most of us a winter visitor only, a few redwings breed in the north of Scotland.*

Left: *A song thrush removes a faecal sac from her offspring. It will be deposited some way from the nest.*

Above: *The robin's juvenile plumage only lasts for a few weeks, before moulting into the familiar red-breasted pattern (right).*

Below: *A robin postures in display, flaring the feathers on its throat. Both sexes hold territory in winter as well as summer.*

Kestrel *Falco tinnunculus*

☐ **Status** Resident. Distributed throughout the British Isles. Some Continental birds appear in winter.

☐ **Habitat** Any sort of country where nest sites can be found; consequently scarce in the Fens.

☐ **Identification** Pigeon sized; long-winged and long-tailed. Male has grey head and tail, which has a black terminal band; wing-tips black; red-brown back spotted with black; underparts buff, with black spots. Female's upper parts red-brown, barred with black; underparts rich buff, brown spotted. Wing-tips dark. Bill and legs yellow. Juvenile similar to female. Length 35 cm (14 in).

☐ **Behaviour** Frequently hovers, head into wind, searching ground for prey. Eats voles, mice, rats and beetles, and small birds in towns; hunts on motorway verges. Flight is pigeon-like, with frequent glides; also circles, when it can look like a sparrowhawk.

☐ **Voice** 'Kee-kee-kee-kee', usually only heard in breeding season.

☐ **Nesting** A scrape on a ledge of a cliff or high building, a tree hole or an old crow's nest. Lays mid-April to May; one brood; three to five white eggs with red-brown blotching; incubation about twenty-eight days, mainly by female. Nestlings fly after twenty-seven to thirty days.

☐ **General notes** Quite common in towns and suburbs. Often seen from gardens, which it may hover over or visit to catch sparrows. Sometimes hunts from perch, dropping on to beetles or crickets below. Will use apple-box sized open-fronted nest box erected 3–6 m (10–20 ft) high on pole or side of building. Top of box should be weatherproofed with overhang; prime with peat.

Pheasant *Phasianus colchicus*

☐ **Status** Resident. Introduced from Caucasus at least 900 years ago. Distributed throughout the British Isles.

☐ **Habitat** Farmland with copses and hedges, woodland edge, parks, large gardens, reed beds and rough grazing.

☐ **Identification** Large, with extremely long tail. Male has bottle-green head and neck; sometimes with white neck-ring; red wattle; green 'ears'; underparts iridescent: mainly chestnut with crescent markings, tail similar but barred. Female mottled brown, shorter tail. Bill horn; legs blue-black. Young birds are like a female with a short tail. Length: male 85 cm (34 in); female 58 cm (23 in).

☐ **Behaviour** Feeds near field edges on animal and vegetable matter, especially fond of grain. Walks sedately; runs from danger unless surprised when it bursts into the air, whirring then gliding on down-turned wings. Roosts in trees.

☐ **Voice** 'Korr-kok', accompanied with wing flapping that can be heard over long distances. When alarmed 'ku-kuk,ku-kuk' repeated rapidly, before flight.

☐ **Nesting** A hollow lined with grass and dead leaves in the shelter of a hedge bottom, bramble-patch, plantation edge, etc. Lays in early April to June; one brood; eight to fifteen eggs, roundish and olive; incubation twenty-two to twenty-seven days. Fluffy young leave nest at a few hours old, and fly at twelve to fourteen days.

☐ **General notes** Will visit garden for grain, and may nest in hedge-bottom bordering farmland or in dense shrubbery. Population reinforced by game-rearing. Survives on waste-ground in towns.

Moorhen *Gallinula chloropus*
☐ **Status** Resident. Distributed throughout the British Isles.
☐ **Habitat** Ponds, slow streams and rivers, lake and marshes.
☐ **Identification** Slightly smaller than pigeon; dumpy body on long legs, very long toes. Brown-black above; blue-black below, with conspicuous white area under tail, and white streaks on edge of flanks. Bill and 'shield' red; legs green. Sexes similar. Juvenile brown. Length 33 cm (13 in).
☐ **Behaviour** Swims across open water with jerky movements. White undertail noticeable. Picks at water surface for vegetable and animal matter. On land treads carefully, tail flicking continuously. Will graze lawns. If disturbed runs for cover. On water, patters across surface, rarely flying when legs dangle; wing-beats fast. Often roosts in waterside trees.
☐ **Voice** Loud, liquid, 'kurruc', 'kittic' and harsh 'kaak'.
☐ **Nesting** Builds nest of water plants on clump of emergent vegetation, attached to overhanging branch, or in tree or bush. Lays from late March to July; two or three broods; five to eleven buff eggs with red-brown speckling; incubation nineteen to twenty-two days, by both parents. Young swim after two or three days.
☐ **General notes** Generally keeps close to cover in gardens, but will graze riverside lawns. Will take food on ground, especially bread or fatty scraps, sometimes flying up on to bird table. Aggressive. Juveniles of first brood will assist care of second brood before dispersing in late autumn.

Herring gull *Larus argentatus*
☐ **Status** Resident. Breeds on coast from Humber round Scotland to Cumbria, Wales, Ireland, West Country and along south coast to Dover; inland at one site in the Pennines. British and Continental birds move freely outside breeding season. Numerous.
☐ **Habitat** Coastal during breeding season. Visits rubbish dumps and fields in winter, including playing fields. Roosts on water at night.
☐ **Identification** Large; bigger than a pigeon. Grey back and wings; white head, tail and underparts; wing-tips black with white 'mirrors'; yellow bill with red spot; pink legs. Sexes similar. Immatures mottled brown. Length 55 cm (22 in).
☐ **Behaviour** Opportunist scavenger, picking animal scraps from water surface or searching beach or ground for dead or live prey. Flight is steady, with shallow wing-beats. Often flies in V-formation when going to roost.
☐ **Voice** The classic 'sea-gull' call – 'keeow' and 'kak,kak,kak'.
☐ **Nesting** Large nest of grass, seaweed, heather or other local material is built on cliff ledge, the ground, or the flat part of a roof in a coastal town. Colonial. Lays mid-April to June; one brood; three olive eggs, blotched with dark brown; incubation about twenty-four days, by both parents. Young fly after six weeks.
☐ **General notes** Population still increasing, but rate of increase slowing down. Town dwelling birds will seize scraps from gardens. Winter birds will visit feeding stations especially in towns. Wary.

Black-headed gull *Larus ridibundus*

☐ **Status** Resident, breeding across most of Ireland, Scotland, Wales and England north of the Wash. South of this, it is more coastal, not breeding in the West Country. Common throughout the British Isles in winter, when it is joined by Continental birds.

☐ **Habitat** Breeds on low-lying coasts and salt marshes, moors and islands in lakes. Outside the breeding season also seen on rivers, sewage farms, rubbish dumps and farmland.

☐ **Identification** Pigeon sized; fairly long wings, tail and legs. In summer has chocolate-brown 'hood'; white underparts and tail; grey back and wings; wing-tips black with white leading edge; bill and legs dark red; in winter loses 'black' head. Sexes similar. Immatures browner, with black band across the tail and dark patch behind ear. Length 35 cm (14 in).

☐ **Behaviour** Active and agile, with faster wing-beats than other gulls. Twists and dives in flight to take food – any scraps, live and dead animal matter and grain. Wanders around at low tide probing, and also follows the plough. Will hover with rapid wing-beats before dropping on food. Roosts on water.

☐ **Voice** Harsh 'kwaar'. Raucous at breeding colonies.

☐ **Nesting** Builds nest of vegetation on ground. Colonial. Lays mid-April to July; one brood; usually five olive-buff eggs, blotched dark brown; incubation is about twenty-three days, by both parents. Young leave nest after a few days, and fly within five to six weeks.

☐ **General notes** Many visit towns in winter, taking food scraps on ground in parks and open gardens. Fairly tame where regularly fed, for example in London parks.

Stock dove *Columba ocnas*

☐ **Status** Resident. Breeds throughout the British Isles except north Scotland; northern and western isles.

☐ **Habitat** Open country, parks, cliffs and dunes.

☐ **Identification** A little smaller than a wood pigeon, with which it can be confused, but lacks white neck-patch; no white on wings; distinguished from feral pigeon by lack of white rump. Overall grey, pinky purple breast suffusing into belly; green neck-patch. Two small, dark bars on inner wing; legs and bill pink; cere (fleshy base of bill) white. Sexes similar. Length 33 cm (13 in).

☐ **Behaviour** Colonial during breeding, but flocks afterwards. Feeds almost exclusively on farmland, sometimes in parks. Mainly grain and seed eater. Glides with raised wings during display flight. Less 'explosive' than wood pigeon on take-off.

☐ **Voice** Deep, throaty 'ooh-ooh-*roo*' with accent on last syllable. Almost a growl.

☐ **Nesting** Typical nest site is a hole in a tree, cliff, sand pit, building, or a nest box (see below). Occasionally a rabbit burrow is used. Colonial. Lays late March to September; two or three broods; two white eggs; incubation about seventeen days, by both sexes. Young fledge in twenty-eight days.

☐ **General notes** Not generally a garden feeder, but may nest in a large garden with old trees or in a nest box with 20 cm (8 in) hole, 37.5 cm (15 in) high, 62.5 cm (25 in) wide and 62.5 cm (25 in) deep. May also use owl or kestrel nest box. Will feed on leftover scraps and brassicas.

Feral pigeon *Columba livia*

☐ **Status** Resident throughout British Isles, especially in towns. Coastal birds in west of Ireland, north and west Scotland and northern isles may be pure rock dove. Descendants of domestic pigeon, whose ancestor was the rock dove.

☐ **Habitat** Towns, coastal cliffs and adjacent farmland.

☐ **Identification** Description is for rock dove, but has many variants. Same size as stock dove, which it also resembles, but has white rump, two dark bars on wing extending nearly to carpal joint, and darker head and neck; white beneath wings; bill dark; legs pink. Sexes similar. Length 33 cm (13 in).

☐ **Behaviour** Frequently seen in display, when male puffs out chest and bows to female. Feeds on ground; heavily dependent on man in winter for scraps, feeding on seed on waste ground in summer and autumn. Also visits farmland for grain and weed seeds. Direct flight strong and fast; climbs and glides in display; claps wings.

☐ **Voice** Tri-syllabic bubbling coo, with accent on middle part.

☐ **Nesting** Builds twig and grass nest in building or cave on ledge, or under eaves, sometimes in loose colonies. Lays March to September; two to four broods; usually two white eggs; incubation is about eighteen days, by both parents. Young fly after about thirty-six days.

☐ **General notes** The rock dove is now so interbred, even in the Artic and Himalayas, it is doubtful whether a pure-bred bird could be identified with certainty. In time, the domestic version will possibly revert to type. At present any colour and variety of shape is possible. Feeds freely in gardens, eating scraps and seeds. This bird needs no encouragement to nest.

Wood pigeon *Columba palumbus*

☐ **Status** Resident and numerous. Widely distributed across the British Isles. Numbers reinforced in winter by Continental immigration.

☐ **Habitat** Farmland, woodland, parkland and suburbs.

☐ **Identification** The largest pigeon, but with a relatively small head. Grey upperparts, with a paler rump; wing-tips and tail dark; broad white

Pigeons drink with a sucking action – unlike most birds which drink with a 'sip and tilt' action.

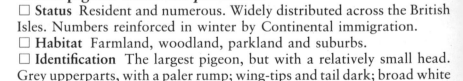

band across wing; small, conspicuous green-and-white neck-patches; breast pink suffusing into pale belly; tip of bill yellow, base red; legs pink. Sexes similar. Juvenile lacks white on neck; pale bill. Length 39 cm (15 in).

☐ **Behaviour** Feeds in flocks on farmland, taking grain, green crops and ripening corn. Also frequents town parks and gardens, where it will take bread and other scraps offered. May raid garden for peas, beans and brassicas. Wary in country, but often tame in towns. Has undulating display flight; clapping wings over back on rise, gliding on descent. Other displays involve 'billing and cooing' (mutual caressing with bill, whilst cooing). Drinks with continuous action, unlike most 'sip and tilt' songbirds.

☐ **Voice** 'Co-coo-*coo*,coo-coo' repeated several times, sometimes abruptly halted in mid-song; accent on third syllable, can sound wheezy.

☐ **Nesting** Builds flimsy twig platform in tree, occasionally elsewhere. Lays April to September; three broods; two white eggs; incubation seventeen days, by both sexes. Young fledge after sixteen to twenty-one days.

☐ **General notes** May become regular at feeding station in town, irregular garden visitor elsewhere; more likely to come to vegetable garden in season. Often breeds late, taking advantage of harvest. Serious crop pest.

Collared dove *Streptopelia decaocto*

☐ **Status** Resident. Widely distributed across British Isles, except on highest ground.

☐ **Habitat** Usually associated with man; occurs in towns, parks, farmyards, docks, especially where there is spilt grain.

☐ **Identification** Small pigeon. Upperparts even buff-brown; underparts pinky buff; thin black-and-white neck-patch; tail black with broad white terminal band (not visible from above); black wing-tips; red eye; grey bill; pink legs. Sexes similar. Length 28 cm (11 in).

☐ **Behaviour** Noisy; usually announces its arrival with flight call. Quite bold on the ground, coming to farmyards and grain stores for spilt grain, and to bird feeders for scraps. Sings from roof-tops and television aerials. Takes off with typical pigeon-like clatter of wings.

☐ **Voice** Harsh 'kwurr' call delivered in flight, often repeated. Song not unlike wood pigeon's but delivered with monotonous rhythm: 'coo-cooo-coo', sometimes only two syllables; accent always on second syllable.

☐ **Nesting** Builds flimsy nest of twigs, grass and roots, usually in conifer or evergreen hedge. Lays March to September, but eggs have been laid in every month of the year; up to five broods; two white eggs; incubation is about fourteen days, by both parents. Fledging occurs after eighteen days.

☐ **General notes** Westward expansion from Balkans started in 1930s; first breeding in Belgium in 1952, England in 1955, Scotland in 1957, Ireland in 1959, Wales in 1961; doubling its population each year in Britain from the first pair in 1955 to an estimated 19,000 in 1964. The rate of expansion has now slowed down. Attracted mainly by grain.

Cuckoo *Cuculus canorus*

☐ **Status** Migrant, occurring from April to September. The bird manages to reach every part of the British Isles except for Shetland.

□ **Habitat** Heaths, moorland, woodland edge, reed beds, farmland.

□ **Identification** Smaller than a pigeon, with long wings and tail. Shape suggests kestrel, colour resembles sparrowhawk; upperparts slate grey, as is head and upper breast; lower breast and belly white barred with grey; wings and tail darker; eye, base of bill and legs yellow. Juvenile and occasional female brown, with brown bars on upperparts (like female kestrel) and underparts. Length 33 cm (13 in).

□ **Behaviour** Elusive; mainly known from its call. On approach, leaves perch with downward motion, flying fast and low with wings below body level, directly towards perch which may be swerved past at last moment before gliding to next suitable perch. Calling is then resumed. Rarely seen feeding, when it drops to ground for caterpillars and insects. Squats on perch.

□ **Voice** Male: 'cuc-koo', usually repeated, sometimes stopped in mid-phrase. Female has long, bubbling note.

□ **Nesting** Lays up to thirteen eggs at forty-eight hour intervals in nests of host: usually meadow pipit, dunnock, reed warbler, robin or pied wagtail, taking egg of host at the same time. Young cuckoo ejects remaining eggs or young soon after hatching – after about thirteen days. Fledges after twenty-one days, fed for further fourteen days by hosts before dispersing.

□ **General notes** Often heard from gardens; may enter in search of hosts. Juveniles sometimes appear in suburbs, migrating at least a month after adults. Takes hairy caterpillars (unlike most insect-eaters). Feet arranged like woodpecker's – two toes facing forward and two toes facing back.

Barn owl *Tyto alba*

□ **Status** Resident and scarce. Uneven distribution; absent from parts of Scotland, rare elsewhere; generally scarcer in east.

□ **Habitat** Needs farm buildings, church towers, ruins or hollow trees for nesting. Hunts over meadows, rough grazing, marshes and road verges.

□ **Identification** Quite large; appears long and slim when perched; large round head and long wings prominent in flight. Upperparts warm buff, finely speckled; face and underparts white; a few speckles on flanks; eyes dark; bill horn; legs feathered and white; claws appear dark. Sexes similar. Length 35 cm (14 in).

□ **Behaviour** Roosts in building or hole by day, hunting mostly at night. Usual strategy is methodical quartering of field or 'beat', with frequent hovering; drops on to prey with legs and feet outstretched. Catches mainly voles, rats and mice. More commonly seen at dusk or dawn when feeding young.

□ **Voice** A blood-curdling wail. At nest, hissing, snoring and bill clacking can be heard.

□ **Nesting** Lays April to July; one or two broods; four to six white eggs laid on pellets on ledge in building or hole in tree or cliff; incubation about thirty-three days, by female only. Young fly after nine to twelve weeks.

□ **General notes** Not really a garden bird, but may be encouraged to nest in outhouse or barn by provision of nest box (see page 58). Increasingly forced on to marginal land. Loss of meadows and unploughed field headlands affecting numbers of prey, demolition of old barns, felling of dead trees, etc. also reduces available nest sites. Specially protected by law.

Little owl *Athene noctua*

☐ **Status** Resident. Introduced from Europe at the end of the last century, now widespread throughout England and Wales. Scarcer in north, and largely absent from Scotland. Not known in Ireland or Isle of Man.

☐ **Habitat** Farmland with trees and hedgerows.

☐ **Identification** Starling sized; typical dumpy owl shape, with flat-topped head; fairly long wings; wing-tips 'fingered' in flight. Upperparts dark brown with pale spots; underparts pale with dark brown streaks; facial 'disc' pale; eyes and bill yellow; legs feathered; feet dark. Sexes similar. Length 22 cm (8½ in).

☐ **Behaviour** Hunts mainly at dusk and dawn, but may be seen at any time. Sits on post or branch, waiting to drop on to prey of beetles, worms, small rodents; occasionally small birds. Bobs head, stretches neck when disturbed before dropping off perch, leaving with bounding flight. Generally roosts outside nest hole on branch; has excellent camouflage.

☐ **Voice** A plaintive 'kiew', and yapping notes.

☐ **Nesting** Nests in hole, usually in tree; also walls, cliffs and burrows; sometimes inside buildings. Lays April to May; usually one brood; three to five white eggs; incubation about twenty-eight days, by female only. Young fly after about twenty-eight days; may be fed by parents for another week.

☐ **General notes** Will use hole-type nest box attached to tree or wedged in ivy-clad wall; hole 10 cm (4 in) min., 30 cm (12 in) high, 25 cm (10 in) wide, 15 cm (6 in) deep. Not unusual near gardens or around farmhouses; may come to outside light to catch moths.

Tawny owl *Strix aluco*

☐ **Status** Resident. Widely distributed in England, Wales and Scotland (except extreme north-west). Absent from Ireland.

☐ **Habitat** Woodland, parks and well-timbered gardens, and farmland with trees.

☐ **Identification** Large owl; usually looks dumpy when perched; stretches up when alarmed; large head. Upperparts brown; mottled and streaked, underparts warm buff, streaked and finely barred with darker brown; facial disc grey-buff; eyes dark; bill horn; legs feathered; claws dark. Sexes similar. Overall tone may vary from very dark brown to tawny or chestnut; sometimes greyish. Length 38 cm (15 in).

☐ **Behaviour** Usually reveals its presence with familiar 'hoot'. Usually hunts from perch, catching mice, rats, often small birds in suburbs, at night. Fishes, frogs and bats are also taken. Flight is direct, the owl disappearing quickly into the night.

☐ **Voice** The call is 'ke-wick', often repeated. The song is a hoot 'hoo-hoo-hoooooooo' the last part about four quavering syllables. Commonly heard at night, also dusk, dawn, occasionally during day, especially late afternoon in December. Hoots in late autumn and early winter when establishing territory; also between March and May when breeding. Young have persistent 'ke-serp' call.

☐ **Nesting** Nests in hole of tree, sometimes old nest of crow, magpie or squirrel; also chimney type nest box (see page 58). Lays March to May; one brood; two to four white eggs; no nest material; incubation twenty-eight to thirty days, by female only. Young fledge after about twenty-eight days.

☐ **General notes** Nests freely in town squares and gardens with suitable trees; often using large hole nest boxes or 'chimneys'. Is aggressive in defence of nest site. Large fluffy young should be put in cover if found, and left for parents to feed.

Swift *Apus apus*

☐ **Status** Migrant, occurring late April to early September. Widespread throughout the British Isles, but scarce in north-west Scotland. Absent in Orkney and Shetland.

☐ **Habitat** Mostly aerial, but needing buildings as nest sites. May congregate over open water or marshes.

☐ **Identification** Not small; almost invariably in flight, generally higher than swallows and martins; streamlined appearance, with scythe-shaped wing pattern and short, forked tail. Sooty brown all over except for whitish patch on throat; generally appears all black. Sexes similar. Length 18 cm (7 in).

☐ **Behaviour** Feeds, mates, preens and even sleeps on the wing; never comes to ground by choice. Cannot perch, but clings to masonry before entering nest hole. Feeds on flying insects, mainly flies. Flight is fast, with rapid wing-beats on stiff wings between glides. Forms 'screaming parties', hurtling around roof tops and low over gardens – when rushing of air can be heard – screaming frequently.

☐ **Voice** A piercing screech, sometimes preceded by a rapid chirruping.

☐ **Nesting** A few items collected on the wing form the 'nest', usually in a roof space, occasionally a tree or cliff hole. Lays May to June; one brood; two to three white eggs; incubation about nineteen days, by both parents. Young fledge at five to six weeks, leaving nest and commencing migration immediately.

☐ **General notes** Heavily dependent on man for nest sites. Usually parasitized by lice –harmless to man – which die before return to Africa. Larvae remain in nest to hatch on swift's return.

Kingfisher *Alcedo atthis*

☐ **Status** Resident. Widely distributed across England, Wales and Ireland. Uncommon in Scotland. May move to coast in winter.

☐ **Habitat** Rivers, streams, lakes and marshes.

☐ **Identification** Quite small; stumpy body, short wings and tail. Brilliant turquoise back, crown and cheek, orange breast and flanks, with broad orange stripe through eye; white chin and neck patch; legs red; long, stout bill dark horn; lower mandible of female red near base. Length 17 cm (6½ in).

☐ **Behaviour** Generally seen flying low and direct over a watercourse, away from the observer. Perches on branch overlooking water, diving for

An access slit cut to allow entry from under the eaves will be appreciated by swifts. A nest box placed over the slit restricts movement and prevents them flying all round the loft. Details for the construction of a nest box are given on page 57.

minnows, sticklebacks, tadpoles, etc. Sometimes hovers before diving.
☐ **Voice** A shrill piping whistle. Song is a trilling version of call.
☐ **Nesting** Excavates 60–75 cm (24–30 in) long tunnel in vertical river bank, occasionally quarry face or sand bank away from water. Lays April to August; two broods; six or seven glossy white eggs, almost round; incubation nineteen to.twenty-one days, by both sexes. Young fly after twenty-three to twenty-seven days.
☐ **General notes** Most likely to be encountered in riverside gardens, or those bordering marshes, but will visit ponds in early morning to fish. Needs post or overhanging branch from which to fish. May be induced to breed by creation of artificial bank near water. Kills fish by banging their heads against branch; swallows prey head first. Badly affected by hard winters.

Green woodpecker *Picus viridis*

☐ **Status** Resident. Widely distributed throughout England and Wales; less common but increasing/expanding range in southern Scotland. Absent from the rest of Scotland and Ireland.
☐ **Habitat** Open woodland and parkland – never far from trees, but also found on heaths, meadows and dunes.
☐ **Identification** Quite large; a little bigger than a collared dove; usually seen in typical woodpecker pose on trunk of tree or on ground. Upperparts grey-green, sometimes appearing quite bright; rump is yellow, end of tail black; cheek, throat and rest of underparts pale buff tinged with yellow; crown is red; area around eye black. Male has red moustachial stripe surrounded by black; female black only. Bill grey; eye white; legs black. Juvenile is spotted white on back, barred grey-green on front. Length 30 cm (12 in).
☐ **Behaviour** Frequently feeds on the ground, especially for ants and other insects; also in trees. Yellow rump on ground and in flight noticcable. Undulating flight, three to five wing-beats followed by loss of height with wings held to sides of body. Often vocal.
☐ **Voice** A ringing 'yaffle', like a laugh.
☐ **Nesting** Makes nest hole in trunk of tree. Lays April to May; one brood; five to seven white eggs laid on a few wood chips; incubation about nineteen days, by both parents. Young fly after twenty-one days.
☐ **General notes** Will nest in gardens; also visits to feed on ants on lawns. Takes suet, mealworms, etc. from feeding stations. May attack beehives, fruit and occupied nest boxes. Might use hole nest box with 6 cm (2¼ in) hole, 37.5 cm (15 in) high, 12.5 cm (5 in) wide and 12.5 cm (5 in) deep.

Great spotted woodpecker *Dendrocopos major*

☐ **Status** Resident. Widely distributed throughout mainland Britain except Caithness. Absent from Ireland.
☐ **Habitat** Woodland, parks and gardens, old orchards.
☐ **Identification** Size of song thrush but appears bigger. Striking black-and-white plumage; underparts very pale buff, with red undertail coverts; upperparts black with large white shoulder-patches; white cheek; black crown. Male has red patch on nape. Juveniles have red crown. Bill and legs black. Length 23 cm (9 in).

Dead wood is home to many creatures. Here a great spotted woodpecker extracts a wood-boring insect on the tip of its long, sticky tongue.

□ **Behaviour** Feeds on trunk and large branches of trees, when piebald appearance can blend with dappled shade. Eats insects, tapping at wood to find them. Also hacks open nuts. Undulating flight as in green woodpecker. Drums loudly in spring to proclaim territory by hammering bill on hollow branch; sounds like machine-gun fire.

□ **Voice** 'Kik' usually repeated after two or three seconds.

□ **Nesting** Makes hole in trunk of tree. Lays in May; four to seven white eggs laid on wood-chips; incubation about sixteen days, mainly by female. Fledging occurs about twenty days later.

□ **General notes** Not uncommon bird table visitor, especially for suet, nuts, etc. Also frequently uses gardens during breeding season in suburbs, mainly for feeding; occasionally nesting. Will use hole nest box with 5 cm (2 in) hole, 30 cm (12 in) high, 12.5 cm (5 in) wide and 12.5 cm (5 in) deep.

Lesser spotted woodpecker *Dendrocopos minor*

□ **Status** Resident. Rather locally distributed in England and Wales. Most frequent in southern and central England.

□ **Habitat** Woodland, parks and gardens, old orchards.

□ **Identification** Sparrow sized. Barred black-and-white appearance; underparts very pale buff, some streaking on flanks; upperparts black barred with white; lacks shoulder-patches of great spotted woodpecker; black moustachial stripe on white face; male has red crown, female white. Juvenile a little red on nape. Bill and legs dark grey. Length 15 cm (6 in).

□ **Behaviour** More active than other woodpeckers; feeding on insects among side branches, fluttering from one branch to next, often on underside, in tit-like manner. Drumming is more rapid, but weaker than great spotted woodpecker's, with no after-vibration. Typical bounding flight of woodpecker.

□ **Voice** 'Ki-ki-ki-ki-ki-ki-ki', also 'kik', but gentler than great spotted woodpecker.

□ **Nesting** Excavates hole in soft wood. Lays April to June; one brood; four to six white eggs; incubation about fourteen days, by both parents.

The young woodpeckers fledge after a period of twenty-one days.

☐ **General notes** Elusive bird, but does enter gardens, and may visit feeding station for fat, nuts and fruit. Barred plumage is excellent camouflage in bare branches or leafy shade.

Swallow *Hirundo rustica*

☐ **Status** Migrant, occurring from April to October. Generally distributed across the British Isles, but less common in north-west Scotland. Rare in Shetland.

☐ **Habitat** Rarely far from man and his habitation, feeding over open fields, lakes, rivers, marshes, etc.

☐ **Identification** Not large; very slim appearance when perched; looks bigger in flight, especially when wings spread open and tail fanned; long, deeply forked tail. Upperparts glossy blue-black; underparts warm beige, sometimes with pink flush; red forehead and throat; blackish bill and legs. Female has shorter tail streamers than male. Juveniles shorter still, with less contrasting plumage. Length 19 cm (7$\frac{1}{2}$ in).

☐ **Behaviour** Spends most of the time in flight catching flying insects, but comes to perch when breeding to sing, usually on wire or bare twig. Flight is easy, fast and low, with acrobatic twists and swoops in pursuit of prey. Congregates on wires, etc. in late August and September before migrating, when it may form large roosts in reed beds.

☐ **Voice** Call a high 'tswit-wit-wit', becoming a rapid twitter at times. Alarm call is 'tsink-tsink'. Song is pleasant twitter with trills, as if bird is sucking in air, sometimes delivered in flight.

☐ **Nesting** Builds saucer-shaped nest of mud and grass, lined with feathers, which is attached to a beam in an outhouse, or supported on a ledge; sometimes a porch or similar covered area is used. Lays May to August; two broods; four to six white eggs, heavily speckled with red-brown; incubation about fifteen days, by female. Young fledge at three weeks.

☐ **General notes** Not found in cities, unlike swifts and house martins. May be seen over playing fields or by rivers in towns. Can be encouraged to breed with artificial nest of fired clay or half-coconut attached to beam in outhouse with permanent access.

House martin *Delichon urbica*

☐ **Status** Migrant, occurring from April to October. Generally distributed across the British Isles, but less common in north-west Scotland. Rare in Orkney and Shetland.

☐ **Habitat** The air over towns, villages, edges of woods and water. Rarely far from habitation.

☐ **Identification** Smaller than a sparrow; dumpy black-and-white bird with white rump; 'triangular' shape in flight. Upperparts glossy blue-black, with conspicuous white rump; dark forked tail; underparts white; no chin strap like sand martin; undersides of wings and tail dark; stubby black bill, white feathered feet and claws. Sexes similar. Length 13 cm (5 in).

☐ **Behaviour** Fluttery flight, with frequent stalls and turns, catches insects in air. Generally feeds at intermediate height between swallows and swifts. Loosely colonial, may be seen in groups on ground at puddles, collecting mud for nests. Gathers with swallows before migration, twittering excitedly.

☐ **Voice** Call is 'tchirrup', often repeated. Alarm call a shrill 'tseep'. Song is a chirruping twitter, rather muted, often delivered from nest.

☐ **Nesting** Builds nest of mud lined with feathers under eaves of building; occasionally on cliffs. Lays May to August; two or three broods; four or five white eggs; incubation about fourteen days, by both sexes. Young fly after about twenty-one days.

☐ **General notes** See text regarding nesting. Has colonized cities as air pollution has decreased.

Sand martin *Riparia riparia*

☐ **Status** Migrant, occurring from March-September. Distribution as for house martin, but does breed in northern isles.

☐ **Habitat** By rivers and reservoirs; cliffs, railway cuttings and working sand-pits.

☐ **Identification** Small; shape of wings more like swallow's than house martin's; forked tail, usually seen in flight. Upperparts sandy-brown; underparts white with brown chin-strap; underside of wings and tail brown, slightly translucent; bill blackish; feet brown. Sexes similar. Length 12 cm (4½ in).

☐ **Behaviour** Flies low and fast over water, hawking for insects; flutters about the sky in house martin fashion near colonies. Gregarious. Clings to outside of nest hole before entering. Will gather on wires in late summer.

☐ **Voice** Call is a dry 'tchirrip'. Alarm sounds like 'brrit'. Song is a dry twittering, delivered in flight.

☐ **Nesting** Excavates 60–90 cm (24–36 in) tunnel in sand bank; nest chamber lined with grass and feathers. Lays May to August; two broods; four to five white eggs; incubation about fourteen days, by both parents. Young fly at about nineteen days.

☐ **General notes** Most likely to be seen near gardens bordering rivers, or near sand or gravel-pits. I have seen a pair nesting in a drain pipe on the bank of a riverside garden. Elsewhere sand banks have been created or cliff-faces excavated for them. Holes 5 cm (2 in) in diameter drilled into banks or cuttings may tempt them.

Carrion crow *Corvus corone*

☐ **Status** Resident. Widely distributed across the whole British Isles, although north-west Scotland, northern and western islands and Ireland have separate form, known as hooded crow, which may be seen in eastern England in winter.

☐ **Habitat** All kinds of open country, town parks and squares with gardens.

☐ **Identification** Large; bigger than a pigeon. All black. Hooded crow has grey back and belly. Bill and legs black. Sexes similar. Length 45 cm (18 in).

☐ **Behaviour** Mainly solitary, or seen in pairs patrolling close to ground on look-out for food. Feeds mainly on ground on all kinds of live and dead

animal matter, also grain, etc. Flight more ragged than rook's, when squarer wings and end of tail help to distinguish it from rook. Hops and walks on ground.
☐ **Voice** 'Kaaah-kaaah-kaaah', and in flight' 'keerk' – a higher note.
☐ **Nesting** Builds substantial nest of twigs high in tree, on cliff, occasionally on building. Lays April to May; one brood; three to five light blue eggs, spotted dark grey-brown; incubation about nineteen days, by female. Fledging occurs after thirty to thirty-five days.
☐ **General notes** Will visit ground feeding station for any scraps, mainly at country gardens, when presence will deter other birds. Wary of man, however, so unlikely to come close to house. Will nest in tree in large garden.

Rook *Corvus frugilegus*
☐ **Status** Resident. Found in all parts of the British Isles except treeless moors.
☐ **Habitat** Farmland with trees for nesting.
☐ **Identification** Large; slightly smaller than carrion crow; wedge-shaped tail. All black except for bare area around base of bill (which juvenile lacks); bill horn tending to black towards tip; legs and feet black, but thighs are feathered, giving 'trousered' look; plumage glossier than crow's. Sexes similar. Length 45 cm (18 in).
☐ **Behaviour** Gregarious at all times, often feeding socially with jackdaws or in loose flocks including pigeons and lapwings. Feeds mainly on invertebrates, also some grain. Walks and hops on ground. Noisy at breeding colonies and in flight, when wing-beats are faster than crows.
☐ **Voice** 'Caw', sometimes repeated. Also higher note more like gull's.
☐ **Nesting** Builds nest of sticks and mud high in tree tops, in colonies of three or four up to 9000. Lays March to April; one brood; three to six pale blue-green eggs; incubation about eighteen days, by female only. Fledging occurs thirty days later.
☐ **General notes** Unlikely to nest in any but the largest gardens with mature trees, but quite common visitor to country gardens taking scraps from ground. Also mingles with crows at rubbish-dumps. Wary.

Jackdaw *Corvus monedula*
☐ **Status** Resident. Widely distributed across British Isles. Less common in Outer Hebrides.
☐ **Habitat** Cliffs, quarries, ruins, parks and open fields.
☐ **Identification** Quite large; smaller than a pigeon with more compact shape. Appears all black in flight; on ground black cap and face contrast with grey nape; rest of plumage black with greyish sheen; bill and legs black; eye pale. Proportionately shorter wings than crows and rooks. Sexes similar. Length 33 cm (13 in).
☐ **Behaviour** Feeds on ground with typical jaunty walk, stopping to probe for grain or animal matter. Often occurs in flocks with rooks and starlings. Flight acrobatic around nest site, faster wing-beat than rook. Vocal.
☐ **Voice** Call a 'chack', sometimes running into 'chaka-chaka-chack'. Also 'kya'.

□ **Nesting** A pile of sticks in a hole or chimney; usually colonially on ruin, cliff or in old parkland trees. Lays April to May; one brood; three to six light blue eggs with black spots; incubation about eighteen days, by female. Young fly after thirty days.

□ **General notes** Commonest crow at bird feeding stations. May come in groups to take scraps, berries, grain, etc. May nest in chimney or hole nest box with 15 cm (6 in) hole, 42 cm (16½ in) high, 19 cm (7½ in) wide and 19 cm (7½ in) deep. Also open kestrel-type nest box or owl 'chimney'.

Magpie *Pica pica*

□ **Status** Resident. Rarely seen outside breeding range which is expanding. Scarce in parts of East Anglia, the Borders and eastern Scotland. Unknown in central and north-west Scotland. Ireland was colonized from twelve birds that were blown over by a storm in 1676.

□ **Habitat** Mainly farmland with trees and bushes; increasingly town suburbs.

□ **Identification** Large; unmistakeable black-and-white crow-sized bird, with long black tail; in flight short, rounded wings contrast with long tail. Closer inspection shows that head, breast and back and wings are glossy blue-black, with white belly and wing-patch; undertail coverts black; tail iridescent green and purple; bill and legs black. Sexes similar. Length 46 cm (18 in).

□ **Behaviour** Shy in the country; bold in towns but always wary. Flight weak, with a few flaps interspersed with a swooping glide. Walks or hops on ground, with tail often held up, sometimes cocked. Eats all kinds of animal and vegetable matter. Infamous as raider of nests and eggs. Sometimes occurs in small groups. Vocal in spring.

□ **Voice** A squeaky 'kyack', often followed by rattling 'chak-ak-ak-ak'.

□ **Nesting** Builds domed twig nest in a tree, occasionally a thorn bush, lined with mud. Lays April to early June; one brood; four to seven light green eggs, speckled grey-brown; incubation about twenty-one days, by female only. Young fledge at thirty days.

□ **General notes** Increasing as a result of lessened persecution by gamekeepers. A threat to young birds and eggs. Visits feeding stations, taking large scraps away. Offering only small food items may deter these and other 'problem' visitors.

Jay *Garrulus glandarius*

□ **Status** Resident. Continental birds winter in some years. Widely distributed across England and Wales, but local in Scotland south of Aberdeen and absent north of there. Thinly distributed in Ireland; absent far north and west.

□ **Habitat** Woodland and parks, large gardens in suburbs.

□ **Identification** Pigeon sized, but larger head and neck. Predominantly pink and black; short, rounded wings and white rump show in flight; upperparts rufous pink, with black wing-tips; white patch on wing with pale blue and black flash on leading edge of wing; rump white; tail black; chin white; rest of underparts pink; black moustache; bill black; legs pink; eyes pale blue. White crown streaked with black, which erects as crest. Sexes similar. Length 35 cm (14 in).

□ **Behaviour** Shy, often only seen flying across clearing or garden, when broad wings beat jerkily, as if bird is in danger of losing height. More woodland based than other crows, feeding on ground on acorns in autumn which it also stores. Hops on ground and in trees, searching for animal and vegetable food, but less of a scavenger than other crows. Takes eggs and nestlings in spring. Sometimes occurs in noisy parties.
□ **Voice** A loud screeching 'skaak, skaak', also harsh or ringing notes.
□ **Nesting** Builds nest of twigs in tree. Lays April to June; one brood; three to six olive-green eggs with darker olive freckles; incubation about sixteen days, by female only. Fledging occurs after twenty days.
□ **General notes** May be tame in some suburban areas, when it will visit bird tables for smaller items than other crows, particularly nuts.

Jays are particularly fond of nuts and sunflower seeds, and many are now regular garden feeding station visitors.

Great tit *Parus major*
□ **Status** Resident. Widely distributed throughout the British Isles except the western and northern isles.
□ **Habitat** Primarily deciduous woodland; also common in gardens and parks.
□ **Identification** A little smaller than a sparrow, but less chunky, and with black-and-yellow appearance. Upperparts greenish-blue, closed wing appearing almost black; head and chin black; cheek white, tail as wings with white outer tail feathers; breast and belly yellow, with black stripe extending from chin to vent; undertail coverts white; white wing-bar obvious in flight. Female's chest stripe narrower and shorter than male's. Juveniles have yellow cheek; dull version of adult plumage. Length 14 cm (5½ in).
□ **Behaviour** Agile and acrobatic, fluttering about trees in search of insects, also hopping on ground for vegetable matter and invertebrates in leaf-litter. Aggressive at feeders. Flight, as with other tits, in fluttering bounds, from one tree to another. Vocal.
□ **Voice** Bewildering variety of calls, of which commonest is 'teacher-teacher-teacher'. Also 'tchair', and chaffinch like 'tsink'.
□ **Nesting** Builds substantial lining of moss, hair, grass and feathers to hole in tree or wall, commonly nest box. Lays April to May; one brood;

eight to twelve white eggs with red-brown spots; incubation about fourteen days, by female only. Young leave after twenty-one days.

☐ **General notes** Common garden bird, although may absent itself in late summer until winter. Nest box user par excellence, also frequent bird table visitor, especially for hanging peanuts. May raid milk bottles.

Blue tit *Parus caeruleus*

☐ **Status** Resident. Widely distributed throughout British Isles except Orkney and Shetland.

☐ **Habitat** Woods, parks and gardens.

☐ **Identification** Small; active blue and yellow bird. Underparts yellow with dark streak on belly; crown, wings and tail blue; back yellow-green; white cheeks with dark eye-stripe, chin-strap and bib; bill dark; legs blue-black. Sexes similar. Juvenile has yellow cheek; duller plumage. Length 12 cm (4½ in).

☐ **Behaviour** Active, rarely staying still for more than a few moments. Often hangs upside down, searching undersides of leaves for caterpillars or pecking at peanuts on hanging feeder. Flight as great tit, only weaker. Butterfly display flight, with rapid fluttering interspersed with gliding on outstretched wings. Calls often while feeding in trees, or aggressive chatter when approaching feeder.

☐ **Voice** Call 'tsee-tsee-tsee-tsit', and a scolding 'churr'. Song starts with call then goes into trill.

☐ **Nesting** Hole-nester of catholic taste. Floor of hole lined with hair, moss, grass and wool. Lays April to May; one brood; eight to fifteen white eggs, lightly spotted with red-brown; incubation about fourteen days, by female only. Fledging occurs after another twenty-one days.

☐ **General notes** Standard nest box user, regular bird table feeder. Usually the first bird to discover peanuts in a hanging feeder. Like other tits, may abandon gardens in late summer to join roving parties of tits in nearby woodland, returning when the living gets harder. Occasionally attacks items as varied as crocuses, putty and strips of paper. Raids milk bottles. Attracted to gardens by suet, fat and nuts in feeders.

Coal tit *Parus ater*

☐ **Status** Resident. Distributed throughout mainland Britain, but absent from Scottish islands.

☐ **Habitat** Woodland and gardens, usually associated with conifers.

☐ **Identification** Our smallest tit: a little smaller than a blue tit. Upperparts olive-blue, with double wing-bar; underparts warm buff, except for black bib; black crown and neck-stripes forming white nape patch; white cheeks; bill black; legs grey-black. Sexes similar. Juvenile has yellower cheeks and nape than adult. Length 12 cm (4½ in).

☐ **Behaviour** More like great tit than blue tit, quite often feeding on ground, especially beneath beeches in autumn. More often feeds in tree canopy of pines and ornamental conifers than on ground on spiders, catepillars and flies. Shyer than blue and great tits at feeders, and dominated by them. Stores nuts. Flight weak and flitting, like blue tit's.

☐ **Voice** Calls are high 'tsui-tssui' and 'tsee'. Song is 'teechu-teechu-teechu', or 'tchuee-tchuee-tchuee', which is then followed by a trill.

Above: *An old kettle,
with the spout facing
down so that water is
not collected, makes an
ideal nest site for a
spotted flycatcher.*

Left: *A single specimen
of one of the fast-
growing cypresses
provides safe cover for a
dunnock.*

Left: *A handsome cock
pied flycatcher – difficult
to see in the dappled
shade once the leaves
have opened. Listen for
the song towards the end
of April, and provide
plenty of nest boxes, as
these birds owe much of
their current success to
artificial nest sites.*

Right: *Fledgling songbirds produce their droppings ready packaged. This female lesser whitethroat will take the sac away, avoiding an accumulation of droppings that could give the nest away to a predator.*

Right: *The drought in the Sahel region south of the Sahara, where the whitethroat spends the winter, has been blamed for the population crash of this once-abundant summer visitor.*

willow warbler

chiffchaff

blackcap

♂

♀

Left: The only reliable way of separating a willow warbler from a chiffchaff is by their songs. Confusingly, female blackcaps have a brown cap! The male is a fine songster.

Left: Although an unusual visitor to the bird table, the goldcrest is usually quite indifferent to human presence.

Below: A garden warbler brings caterpillars to its hungry nestlings.

Above: *A pied wagtail is a familiar sight in summer.*

Right: *Winter is a more likely time to find a meadow pipit in the garden.*

Below: *Grey wagtails are more closely associated with rivers than are pied wagtails.*

□ **Nesting** Lines hole in tree, or wall (often low down in bank), with moss and hair. Lays April to May; sometimes two broods; six to ten eggs, white speckled red-brown; incubation fourteen days, by female. Fledging occurs about sixteen days later.

□ **General notes** Will use standard nest box in gardens. Numbers less affected by availability of natural tree hole sites because of preference for holes in banks and tree roots. Colonization of new conifer plantations may be rapid. Attracted by seeds and nuts in feeders.

Marsh tit *Parus palustris* and Willow tit *Parus montanus*

□ **Status** Resident. Thinly distributed in England and Wales. Scarce in south-east Scotland (marsh tit), and south-west Scotland (willow tit). Absent from Ireland, and islands off mainland Britain.

□ **Habitat** Deciduous woodland (marsh tit), mixed woodland (willow tit); both sometimes appearing in adjacent gardens, hedgerows, etc.

□ **Identification** Same size as blue tit, although willow tit is bulkier and bull-necked. Both birds have broadly the same plumage with only minor differences: upperparts and tail are grey-brown; black cap and bib; pale buff underparts; bill and legs grey-black; cap of willow tit is sooty, that of marsh tit is glossy; willow tit's bib is bigger than marsh tit's; willow tit has light panel on edge of wing. Song is best way to tell apart. Sexes similar. Length 12 cm (4½ in).

□ **Behaviour** As other tits, but a little less active. Marsh tit often feeds at lower level than willow tit in secondary growth of hazel and hornbeam. Being woodland birds, flight is usually short and obscured, but has same characteristics as blue tit's.

□ **Voice** Both have similar 'tchay' calls, but marsh tit also has 'pitchou' call, whereas willow tit has buzzing 'eez-eez'. Song of marsh tit is bubbling 'shipi-shipi-shipi', while willow tit's song is a rising 'tsee-tsee-tsee', sometimes 'piu', repeated three times.

□ **Nesting** Both use tree holes, but willow tit excavates own hole in rotting alder, willow or birch, occasionally elder. Both lay eggs on pad of animal hair (and moss in case of marsh tit). Lay April to May; one brood (marsh tit sometimes two); six to eight white eggs with red-brown speckles; incubation about fourteen days, by female only. Young fledge after sixteen days.

□ **General notes** Both will use standard nest box, although for willow tit a greater depth (about 5 cm/2 in more) is preferred, and box should be packed with sawdust or polystyrene so that tit makes its own hole. Alternatively introduce soft, rotting stump of birch into garden, strapping it to healthy tree. Birds may nest very low down, so beware predators! Both are locally regular bird table visitors. Eat seeds, nuts and fat.

Long-tailed tit *Aegithalos caudatus*

□ **Status** Resident. Not as numerous as blue tit, but occurs in all of mainland Britain although scarce in south-west Ireland, north-west England and far north of Scotland.

□ **Habitat** Less confined to woodland than other tits: dense thickets, hedgerows, heathland edge as well as woodland and gardens.

☐ **Identification** Small; a ball of feathers with a 7.5 cm (3 in) tail stuck on! Usually reveals itself first with calls. Long black-and-white tail, black wings, nape and back; pink band from shoulders to rump forming V-shape; white crown and cheeks; black stripe over eye; underparts off-white tending towards pink on belly; black bill and legs. Sexes similar. Juvenile duller. Length 14 cm (5½ in).

☐ **Behaviour** Very active, flitting in small parties through secondary growth, calling incessantly to each other. Diet more invertebrate based than that of other tits, especially spiders, but some seeds. Flits across space between trees singly, when easy to count numbers in family party (fourteen not unusual).

☐ **Voice** Contact calls a buzzing 'tsirrrup' and low 'tupp'. Song a mixture of call notes and 'see-see-siu', sung rapidly.

☐ **Nesting** Builds a domed nest of moss, lichens and cobwebs, lined with feathers, often in hawthorn, gorse or beech hedge. Lays late March to May; usually one brood; eight to twelve white eggs capped with red-brown freckles; incubation about fourteen days, mainly by female. Fledging occurs after about fourteen days.

☐ **General notes** Most likely to visit garden with boundary hedge near woodland, scrub or heath, when whole party may visit in hard weather for fat, bird pudding, etc. May nest in suitable hedge. Communal roosting in winter, when prolonged hard weather causes heavy mortality.

Nuthatch *Sitta europaea*

☐ **Status** Resident. Mainly occurs in southern and central England and Wales, although expanding its range and increasing in north-east. Absent from most of Scotland, Ireland and islands off mainland Britain.

☐ **Habitat** Deciduous and mixed woods, parks and gardens with mature trees.

☐ **Identification** Sparrow sized; broad-based, rounded wings; compact grey and pink bird. Upperparts blue-grey; black tail has white corners at tip; black eye-stripe, warm pink-buff underparts, flanks of male chestnut

Nuthatches are often observed walking down a tree trunk.

in spring; stout, pointed bill is black; legs pink. Length 14 cm (5½ in).
☐ **Behaviour** Active tree-dwelling bird, equally at home upside down on the underside of a branch or coming head-first down the main trunk. Hops on ground. Eats mainly nuts, but also caterpillars, earwigs and beetles. Fond of peanuts at bird feeders. Flight is rather woodpecker-like, but often from low down and rising in bounds to nearby tree. Often seen as pair, in all seasons.
☐ **Voice** Varied but distinctive, having same piping quality. Call is ringing 'chwit-chwit', 'tsit' and trilling 'tsirr'. Song is loud trill with 'qui-qui,' repeated a number of times. Also fluty whistling.
☐ **Nesting** Lines tree or wall hole with bark flakes and leaves. Entrance to hole is plastered up with mud to restrict entrance; same habit applying to nest boxes with correct-size hole! Lays April to May; one brood usually; six to eleven white eggs, spotted red-brown; incubation fourteen days, by female only. Fledging occurs after about twenty-four days.
☐ **General notes** Regular bird table visitor in certain areas, and habit increasing. Particularly fond of nuts, but also suet, fats, etc. Hacks open nuts with powerful bill after wedging them in crevice in bark. Nests in suitable gardens.

Treecreeper *Certhia familiaris*
☐ **Status** Resident. Breeds in every county of Britain and Ireland except Orkney and Shetland.
☐ **Habitat** Woodland of all types, and parks and gardens with mature trees.
☐ **Identification** Smaller than sparrow; slight, mouse-like bird with quick movements and flitting flight. Upperparts are mottled mouse-brown; underparts are white, some brownish streaks on flanks; indistinct white eye-stripe; dark eye and bill; legs pink. Sexes similar. Length 12 cm (4½ in).
☐ **Behaviour** Creeps up stems of trees with jerky, spiralling action. At point where side shoots begin often flits down to base of neighbouring tree to repeat same process. Usually solitary, although joins roving flocks of tits in winter. Call is often first indication of presence.
☐ **Voice** Call is a high, thin 'tsee' or 'tsit'. Song is repeated calls with 'tsizzi-tsee' on the end, delivered in a flourish.
☐ **Nesting** Builds untidy nest behind loose piece of bark or similar tree cavity, occasionally behind ivy on wall. Lays April to June; sometimes two broods; usually six white eggs, spotted red-brown; incubation about fifteen days, mainly by female. Young fledge at about twenty-four days.
☐ **General notes** May nest in gardens, particularly those with Wellingtonia. Wedge-shaped box can be provided, on back-plate 15 × 25 cm (6 × 10 in), front at top projects 12.5 cm (5 in), tapering down to base; 5 cm (2 in) wide access hole at top taken out of side panels. May visit nut feeder, or take food (fat, suet, etc.) in bark crevices.

Wren *Troglodytes troglodytes*
☐ **Status** Resident. Widespread throughout the British Isles.
☐ **Habitat** Wherever there is cover – found in woodland, gardens, shrubberies, heathland, moorland, areas of scrub, etc.

☐ **Identification** Very small; active brown bird; round body; cocked tail, slender bill. Upperparts chestnut brown barred with black on wings, flanks and tail; pale stripe over eye; underparts paler buff-brown; bill dark; legs pink. Sexes similar. Length 10 cm (4 in).

☐ **Behaviour** Creeps mouse-like through vegetation or on ground, with more scuttling action than treecreeper. Cocked tail is distinctive. Flies with whirring wings, in a straight line from one clump of undergrowth to the next, only short distances. Feeds almost entirely on insects; a few seeds taken, however. Perches conspicuously on top of bracken frond or bramble to sing, with head up and bill wide open.

☐ **Voice** A harsh 'churr' when alarmed, but usually 'chit-chit'. Song is strident jingle of warbling and trilling notes, amazingly loud for such a small bird.

☐ **Nesting** Male builds several domed nests of grass, leaves and moss, one of which female selects, lining it with feathers; usually fairly low down in creeper, wall crevice, brushwood or in corner of building. Lays April to June; usually two broods; five or six white eggs with red-brown spots; incubation about fourteen days, by female only. Young fly after about sixteen days.

☐ **General notes** Our most widely distributed bird, reaching the outer islands where separate races have evolved. After a series of mild winters also our most numerous bird, but being insectivorous is badly affected by hard winters. Only occasional bird table visitor. Takes grated cheese sprinkled over leaf litter. May use standard nest box.

Mistle thrush *Turdus viscivorus*

☐ **Status** Resident. Widely distributed across the British Isles, breeding in every county except Orkney, Shetland and Outer Hebrides.

☐ **Habitat** Parks, gardens, golf courses, woodland and heathland edge. Found in more open country outside breeding season.

☐ **Identification** Quite large; smaller than a pigeon. Like big version of familiar song thrush, but greyer in appearance and with breast spotted rather than streaked; pale grey-brown above, wings showing pale feather edges; underparts are pale, with some buff on breast and flanks, which are boldly spotted with very dark brown; white underwing conspicuous in flight; bill horn; legs pink. Sexes similar. Juvenile paler than adults. Length 27 cm (11 in).

☐ **Behaviour** Bold and fearless with other birds, attacking larger birds that venture over territory, but shy of man. Feeds mainly on ground, often in family parties, hopping across lawns looking for worms, larvae and snails. Also takes berries and fruits. Flight is quite fast and direct; rising, with a few strong wing-beats interspersed with gliding; not as undulating as woodpecker's. Often calls in flight.

☐ **Voice** Call is rattling 'chrrrrrrrrrr', usually delivered in flight. Song is more fluty than that of song thrush, consisting of repeated phrases. Will sing from exposed perch in February in wind and rain, thus earning the name 'stormcock'.

☐ **Nesting** Builds cup of grass, earth and moss in fork of tree. Lays late February to late May; two broods, four pale blue eggs, splotched red-brown; incubation about fourteen days, by female. Fledging occurs after a period of about fourteen days.

□ **General notes** Will visit ground feeding station with caution for fruit (especially apples), although it will feed and nest in larger gardens. More likely to come to drink.

Parties of fieldfares call to each other in flight to maintain contact.

Fieldfare *Turdus pilaris*

□ **Status** Migrant, occurring from October to April, wintering across the British Isles. A few breed in widely scattered locations, but large-scale colonization seems unlikely.

□ **Habitat** Open farmland, hedgerows. Playing fields and gardens in hard weather.

□ **Identification** Same size as blackbird, although often appears larger. Chestnut-brown back and wings; grey head and rump; black tail; underparts warm orange-buff, speckled black; bill yellow with black tip; legs black; white underwing conspicuous in flight. Sexes similar. Length 25 cm (10 in).

□ **Behaviour** Flocking bird, feeding on open ground, often with redwings. Takes worms and grubs when ground is soft; hops on ground. Often swarms on berry crop when it first arrives. Flight is quite strong, gently undulating, rather like that of a mistle thrush. Calls frequently in flight.

□ **Voice** Call is a rattling 'chack-chack-chack', and a nasal 'see-e'. Song is usually given in flight: a series of chattering, squeaky notes, the bird flying between trees with short, stiff wing-beats. Colonial at breeding sites and aggressive.

□ **Nesting** *Very* rare breeder in Britain. Builds nest of grass, roots and mud in tree or bush. Lays April to June; often two broods; four to seven blue-green eggs with brown or violet spotting; incubation about fourteen days, mainly by female. Fledging also occurs in about fourteen days.

□ **General notes** Increasingly coming to gardens in New Year for fruit, etc. Usually feeds on the ground, but also goes to table for other items. Breeding on Continent increasing in gardens, so colonists may adopt gardens here.

Song thrush *Turdus philomelos*

□ **Status** Resident. Widespread, breeding throughout the British Isles. Continental birds winter here.

□ **Habitat** Parks and gardens, hedgerows with trees, woodland edge.

□ **Identification** Not small; between a starling and a blackbird in size; alert brown-and-white bird with speckled breast, usually seen feeding on lawn. Upperparts are warm brown, including wings and tail; underparts are off-white, speckled with dark brown, some buff on flanks; bill is yellow horn; eye dark; legs flesh-pink. Sexes similar. Length 23 cm (9 in).

□ **Behaviour** Feeds mainly on ground, running then stopping abruptly, head cocked to one side to listen for worms. After a quick stab, the worm is pulled from the ground, and with a few hops the bird flies to the safety of a tree. Breaks snails open using stone as anvil. Also eats berries and seeds. Flight is usually over short distances, rising from ground to nearby perch with rapid wing-beats. Level flight is gently undulating, when pale orange underwing can be seen. Dodges around bushes in flight in the manner of a blackbird.

□ **Voice** Call is a quiet 'chick', repeated louder as alarm, and a 'seep', but shorter in duration than redwing's. Song is repeated phrases, sounding like 'pretty dick, pretty dick; did he do it, did he do it; he did, he did, he did'. Sings in autumn after moult.

□ **Nesting** Builds mud-lined nest of grass and leaves, fairly low in bush or tree, sometimes on ledge in shed. Lays March to July; two or three broods; four to five light blue eggs, lightly speckled with red-brown or black; incubation about fourteen days, by female only. Fledging also about fourteen days.

□ **General notes** Formerly more numerous than blackbird, but apparently harder hit than latter in very cold winters, due to more animal-based diet. Nervous bird table feeder; happier at ground feeding station.

Redwing *Turdus iliacus*

□ **Status** Migrant, occurring from October to April, wintering across the British Isles. Regularly nesting in Scotland since 1953, occasional elsewhere.

□ **Habitat** As fieldfare, although perhaps more associated with woodland.

□ **Identification** A little smaller than a song thrush; clean-looking brown-and-white bird with noticeable red on flanks. Upperparts, wings and tail are rich uniform brown; pale stripe over eye (supercilium) and under dark cheek; underparts clean white, streaked with dark brown; sides of breast have some buff, much paler than rusty-red of flanks and underwing, which is otherwise grey-brown; bill yellow on lower mandible, dark on upper; legs flesh-pink. Sexes similar. Length 21 cm ($8\frac{1}{4}$ in).

□ **Behaviour** Closer to song thrush than fieldfare in general behaviour and appearance; running as well as hopping on ground. Takes worms, etc. from ground; also berries of rowan, hawthorn, etc. when available. Flight often short – from ground to shelter of nearest trees. Long-distance flight is bursts of flickering wing-beats, interspersed with glides. Red underwing visible at a distance. Calls to keep in contact with other flying birds.

□ **Voice** Call is a thin 'seep', often heard at night. Alarm is 'chittuc'. Song (may be heard late winter away from breeding areas) is repeated phrase 'trui-trui-trui-troo-tri', with fluty notes, followed by a warbling subsong.

☐ **Nesting** Regular breeding only in Scotland. Builds cup of earth and twigs, lined with grass, low down near base of tree, in bush or on the ground. Lays mid-May to July; one brood; five to six green-blue eggs with fine red-brown markings, incubation about fourteen days, by both parents. Fledging also occurs after about fourteen days.

☐ **General notes** Will visit ground feeder or table for berries, fruit, etc. Could become garden nesting bird in Scotland!

Blackbird *Turdus merula*

☐ **Status** Resident. Numerous and widespread throughout the British Isles. Continental immigration swells winter population.

☐ **Habitat** Gardens, parks, scrub, woods, hedgerows, etc.

☐ **Identification** Quite large; midway between song thrush and mistle thrush. Male is virtually unmistakeable, being all black (not glossy), with yellow bill and eye-ring, dark eye and legs; tail proportionally longer than other thrushes. Female has dark-brown upperparts, pale throat and dark rust underparts mottled with dark brown; bill is dark, sometimes with yellow or orange at base; yellow eye-ring; dark eye and legs. Juvenile is a paler, more mottled version of female. Length 25 cm (10 in).

☐ **Behaviour** Probably our best-adapted garden bird. Bold; running and hopping on ground to take worms, caterpillars, grubs, etc. and flying up to bushes for soft fruit, or noisily turning over leaf-litter (especially in woods) for seeds and insects. Flies fairly low, often dodging round a bush before landing on open ground with tail raised and wings drooped. Sings loudly from prominent perch; calls noisily at dusk.

☐ **Voice** Call is a low 'tchook'; a persistent 'tchink-tchink' when alarmed, turning into a screeching chatter as the bird takes flight. Arguably our finest songster; song is a mixture of mellow warbling notes, each phrase dying away before the next strong burst of song. Also has a low subsong.

☐ **Nesting** Builds cup of leaves and grass with some mud, in bush, climber or in an outhouse. Lays late March to July; usually two or three broods; three to six light blue-green eggs with red-brown speckles; incubation about fourteen days, by female only. Young fly after a further fourteen days.

☐ **General notes** Familiar, even in the centre of cities. Thrives on garden life, feeding and nesting freely. Aggressive at bird table. Partial albinos not uncommon, complete albinos rare but more likely than any other species.

A typical blackbird pose – listening or looking for a worm.

Redstart *Phoenicurus phoenicurus*

□ **Status** Migrant, occurring from April to September. Scattered distribution in mainland Britain; most common in north and west, although it does not breed in Cornwall or Caithness. Absent from most islands. Very rare breeder in Ireland.

□ **Habitat** Deciduous woods in hill country; also parks with old trees, heathland and moorland edge, especially in stone-wall country. Also found on river banks with pollarded willows and, locally, old orchards and gardens.

□ **Identification** Sparrow sized; shape and behaviour similar to robin. Male has steely-grey back, darker wings and fiery-red tail with dark centre-stripe; crown is grey with white forehead; black throat and face, orange-red breast and flanks; white belly; bill, legs and eye blackish. Female has red tail; grey-brown back and wings; buff underparts; orange on breast. Juvenile as female. Length 14 cm (5$\frac{1}{2}$ in).

□ **Behaviour** Active, restless bird, with habit of repeatedly flicking red tail. Feeds mainly in trees, often high up, flitting from one branch to another, also catching insects in sallies from outer branches, flycatcher style. Drops from low branch to ground to catch prey, then back into tree. Rarely seen to fly long distances; flits short distances from tree top or through foliage.

□ **Voice** Call is a clear 'whee-tic-tic', or 'wheet' in alarm. Song begins rather like chaffinch's, ending with squeaky jangle.

□ **Nesting** Builds nest of grass, lined with hair, in tree or wall cavity, occasionally nest box. Lays May to June; often double brooded; five to eight pale blue eggs, sometimes with red-brown speckles; incubation about fourteen days, by female only. Fledging occurs after about sixteen days.

□ **General notes** Continental counterpart of robin, frequently nesting in gardens on Continent while their robin is a shy woodland bird, more like British redstarts. Will use standard hole nest box, and can be encouraged to nest among conifers (as on Continent) by their provision.

Robin *Erithacus rubecula*

□ **Status** Resident. Widespread and common throughout British Isles except Shetland. Some Continental birds winter here.

□ **Habitat** Gardens, copses and woods, hedgerows and parkland.

□ **Identification** Sparrow sized; familiar, rotund bird; alert and jaunty. Upperparts grey-brown; face and breast red fringed with grey; rest of lower parts off-white tending to buff on lower flanks and undertail coverts; dark, slender bill; dark eye; legs grey-brown. Sexes similar. Juvenile has pale spots on upperparts; underparts mottled buff. Length 14 cm (5$\frac{1}{2}$ in).

□ **Behaviour** Active; dropping from perch to pick up invertebrates from ground, hopping on lawns to pull worms from the ground; also eats seeds and berries. May hover by hanging feeder, sometimes clinging to peck at peanuts in cold weather. Will come readily to freshly turned soil. Erect posture, often with drooped wings. Flight is characterized by rapid wing-beats, and flitting action. Sings almost all year round.

□ **Voice** Call is 'tic', often repeated rapidly. Also a plaintive 'tsee' and 'tsip'. Song is a series of high warbles.

☐ **Nesting** Famed for the variety of its nest sites. Builds bulky nest of moss and dead leaves, lined with hair, well concealed in a hole in a bank, tree stump or in ivy; also in outhouses and open-fronted nest boxes, discarded kettles, etc. Lays March to June; two broods; three to six white eggs, blotched red-brown; incubation about fourteen days. Fledging occurs after twelve to fourteen days.

☐ **General notes** Regular and confiding bird table visitor; a good subject for hand-taming. Britain's national bird.

Robins are justifiably popular, becoming increasingly confiding with familiarity.

Blackcap *Sylvia atricapilla*

☐ **Status** Migrant, occurring from April to October. Widely distributed in England and Wales; scarce breeder in southern Scotland and scattered localities in Ireland. Some Scandinavian birds winter here, mainly in the south-west.

☐ **Habitat** Woodland with good undergrowth, thick shrubberies in parks and gardens (especially rhododendrons), overgrown hedgerows and scrub.

☐ **Identification** Quite small; a little smaller than a sparrow, and slimmer with an insect-eater's slender bill. Only male has black cap; grey-brown upperparts, grey face and nape, extending from throat on to breast, gradually becoming paler. Female is similar, but has chestnut-brown cap (can look almost red in some lights); bill, eye and legs blackish. Juvenile resembles female. Length 14 cm (5½ in).

☐ **Behaviour** Skulking; only occasionally coming to edge of undergrowth to feed or sing. Hops rather heavily through undergrowth, finding insects and caterpillars on the underside of leaves. Occasionally flies out to catch insects in the air. Early arrivals, and autumn and wintering birds, also eat fruit, especially elderberries, and the berries of honeysuckle, ivy, privet and bramble. Flits jerkily across open space, disappearing quickly into cover again. Usually located by song.

☐ **Voice** Call is a hard 'tac-tac' note when cover is approached, turning to a harsh 'churr' if nesting is taking place. Song is a rich warbling, similar to garden warbler's, but generally more liquid, shorter in duration and ending with whistling notes.

☐ **Nesting** Builds grass cup lined with hair and fine grasses low down in dense vegetation, occasionally in tree. Lays May to July; two broods; four to five light buff eggs, marbled brown and grey; incubation about twelve days, by both parents. Young fly in ten to twelve days.

☐ **General notes** Gardens without breeding birds may see migrating or wintering birds, which come increasingly to feeders, especially in shrubby gardens. Migrating birds will feed on autumn fruit.

Garden warbler *Sylvia borin*

□ **Status** Migrant, occurring from April to October. Widely distributed in England, Wales and Scotland north to Inverness, although less common north of the Scottish lowlands. Mainly restricted in Ireland to a band running from Limerick in the south to Lough Erne in the north.

□ **Habitat** Very similar to blackcap's, although perhaps more woodland biased.

□ **Identification** Quite small; slimmer and smaller than a sparrow; has slender bill and warbler's skulking habits; utterly without distinguishing marks, except for dark eye in paler face; clean, neat appearance. Upperparts even grey-brown; underparts paler grey-brown; bill and legs blackish. Sexes similar. Length 14 cm (5½ in).

□ **Behaviour** Best located by its song, which may be delivered from a high perch, affording the observer a view. Generally keeps to thick vegetation, feeding on insects. In autumn feeds more on the outside of shrubs for berries. Flies rapidly to cover with flitting action.

□ **Voice** Very similar calls to blackcap. Song is quieter and more sustained than blackcap's, however, without penetrating whistles.

□ **Nesting** Builds nest of dried grass lined with hair and rootlets, low down in thick cover. Lays late May to June; occasionally two broods; three to six white or pale green eggs, obscured with brown and grey freckles; incubation about twelve days, mainly by female. Young leave nest after ten days.

□ **General notes** Will breed in large shrubbery in garden, more usually seen in autumn coming for berries, or to drink. Despite its lack of distinctive features, is not without character.

Whitethroat *Sylvia communis*

□ **Status** Migrant, occurring from April to September. Widespread throughout the British Isles, becoming more thinly distributed in north-west Scotland.

□ **Habitat** Scrub, heath and hedgerows, woodland edge.

□ **Identification** Approximately sparrow sized, but with typical *Sylvia* warbler shape; rufous bird, with upright pose. Male has rufous upperparts, with white outer tail feathers and grey cap and cheek; white throat; underparts are pink-tinged. Female is similar but lacks grey on head. Bill horn; legs yellowish; light brown eye. Juvenile resembles female. Length 14 cm (5½ in).

□ **Behaviour** Less skulking than most *Sylvia* species, beginning song flight from exposed perch on bush, climbing steeply before dropping back to bush. Otherwise perches erect on edge of bush (especially bramble) to sing, or moves in and out of cover with more horizontal pose. Occasionally raises 'crest' and cocks tail. Feeds on insects, occasionally taken in flight, and berries.

□ **Voice** Call is a nervous 'check', scolding 'charr' and subdued 'wheet-wheet, whit-whit-whit'. Song is scratchy warbling, but quite pleasant.

□ **Nesting** Male builds 'cock's' nests of grasses, female lining that chosen with down and horse hair. Lays May to July; usually two broods; four to five pale green or buff eggs, with grey, mauve or brown markings; incubation about twelve days, by both parents. Young leave after eleven days.

☐ **General notes** May nest in boundary hedge of garden, particularly if bordering scrub or heath. Visits gardens for berries in autumn.

Lesser whitethroat *Sylvia curruca*

☐ **Status** Migrant, occurring from April to September. Restricted mainly to England. Commonest in Midlands and East Anglia, but some in north Wales; few in Devon and Cornwall. Rarely occurs elsewhere, except for a few migrants in eastern Scotland.

☐ **Habitat** Much as whitethroat (but usually with more trees) – orchards, parks and gardens.

☐ **Identification** A little smaller than a whitethroat and greyer; 'masked' appearance. Upperparts grey-brown, with grey head and upper back; indistinct white on outer tail feathers; darker grey 'mask' around eyes; white throat and breast; flanks and belly tending to buff – in male a suffusion of pink; blackish bill and legs; brown eye. Sexes similar. Length 13 cm (5 in).

☐ **Behaviour** More skulking than whitethroat, only occasionally coming to edge of bush. Feeds on insects among foliage, sometimes high in tree; sometimes flies out to catch passing insects. Feeds lower down in autumn, showing a preference for berries, especially elder. Flight is weak and flitting, when it shows shorter tail than whitethroat.

☐ **Voice** Call is an anxious 'tac-tac' and 'charr' of alarm, especially when feeding young. Song is like chaffinch's but without terminal flourish.

☐ **Nesting** Male builds nest of grass, roots and hair, which female lines with down and animal hair, low down in thorny bush, sometimes in a dense conifer. Lays May to July; two broods; four to six off-white eggs, with brown or grey markings; incubation about eleven days, by female mainly. Young leave nest after further eleven days.

☐ **General notes** Not infrequent in gardens within rather restricted range; nesting in shrubberies and boundary hedges; also visiting for berries prior to migration.

Willow warbler *Phylloscopus trochilus*
and Chiffchaff *Phylloscopus collybita*

☐ **Status** Migrants, occurring from April to September (willow warbler); or March to October (chiffchaff). Both widespread across England, Wales and Ireland; willow warbler also in Scotland including Hebrides and Orkney – chiffchaff scarce in Scotland, and absent north of line joining Fort William and Perth. Some chiffchaffs overwinter.

☐ **Habitat** Light woodland, scrub, shrubberies, bushy commons, large gardens. Chiffchaff shows some preference for trees giving a 3.5 m (11½ ft) song post.

☐ **Identification** Smaller than a sparrow; with slim, slender-billed appearance; species are so subtly different that only song can positively identify them. Upperparts olive-brown (willow warbler greener than chiffchaff in spring), with pale supercilium; underparts pale, yellowybuff; bill pale brown (willow warbler), darker in chiffchaff; legs usually pale pink (willow warbler), usually darker in chiffchaff. Juveniles of both species quite yellow below in autumn. Sexes similar. Length 10 cm (4 in).

□ **Behaviour** Both active 'leaf' warblers, spending most of their time feeding on insects in the outer branches of trees, willow warbler feeding in bushes more than chiffchaff. Both will take berries in autumn, especially elderberries and currants. Willow warbler regarded as more active of two. Both birds rarely fly more than a few metres through open branches, with a light, flitting action.

□ **Voice** Calls are similar: willow warbler's 'hoo-eet' and chiffchaff's 'hweet' both doubling as alarms when sounded urgently. Willow warbler's song is light, rippling cascade of notes down the scale, ending with a flourish. Chiffchaff's song, often preceded by 'chuddr-chuddr', is variation on two notes, 'chiff-chaff, chiff-chaff, chiff-chaff, chaff-chaff-chaff', in which 'chaff' is the lower note of the two.

□ **Nesting** Both species build domed nests of moss and dried grasses, lined with feathers, usually on the ground (willow warbler), low in bush or undergrowth (chiffchaff). Lay April to May; sometimes two broods (in case of willow warbler); six to seven white eggs, with red-brown blotches (willow warbler), or purple-brown spots (chiffchaff); incubation about fourteen days, by female only. Young fly after a further fourteen days.

□ **General notes** Both may pass through gardens on migration, occasionally nesting in large gardens with shrubberies or medium-height trees – both species associated with birch trees. Chiffchaff also favours rhododendron undergrowth – especially overwintering birds. Wintering chiffchaffs will come to bird table for crumbs and berries, etc.

Goldcrest *Regulus regulus*

□ **Status** Resident. Widely distributed throughout the British Isles except the Outer Hebrides, Orkney and Shetland.

□ **Habitat** Mixed and coniferous woods, parks and gardens with ornamental conifers; also scrub in winter.

□ **Identification** Very small; dumpy, active bird invariably in trees. Upperparts are dark olive-green; double bar on wing; gold crest on crown flanked either side with black; centre of crown stripe in breeding male is red; underparts greenish-buff; bill, eye and legs blackish. Juvenile resembles female. Length 9 cm ($3\frac{1}{2}$ in).

□ **Behaviour** Lively and fearless of man, feeding unconcernedly low down on outer branches, then flitting high up in foliage, usually of conifer. Searches for insects among leaves and needles, often hovering to reach prey. Subsists on spiders and insect eggs and larvae in winter, when it will form communal roosts for warmth.

□ **Voice** Call is thin, high, 'zee-zee-zee'. Song is equally high 'weedely-weedely-weedely-weedely-wee-e-eet', ending with little flourish.

□ **Nesting** Builds deep hammock-shaped cup of moss and cobwebs, lined with feathers; slung from branch of conifer, usually high up. Lays April to June; two broods; seven to ten eggs with pale ground, speckled with brown; incubation about fifteen days, by female only. Young fly after about twenty-one days.

□ **General notes** Will visit bird table to peck at grated cheese, fine crumbs or fat. Not infrequent garden breeder. Our smallest bird.

Spotted flycatcher *Muscicapa striata*

☐ **Status** Migrant, occurring from May to September. Distributed across the British Isles, including Orkney and the recently colonized Hebrides. Absent from Shetland.

☐ **Habitat** Parks and gardens, woodland edge.

☐ **Identification** A little smaller than a sparrow, with a thin, insect-eater's bill and very upright stance; characterful bird, despite dull plumage. Upperparts are mouse-brown, with pale edges to the wing feathers; crown has slight crest, lightly spotted; underparts are greyish-white, lightly streaked with brown on throat and breast; bill, eye and legs blackish. Sexes similar. Length 14 cm (5½ in).

☐ **Behaviour** Alert, nervous appearance, sitting upright on exposed perch flicking wings and tail. Particularly fond of feeding from dead outer branches of otherwise healthy trees. Flies out from perch to take passing insects, usually returning to same position. Low, swooping flight, with abrupt twists and turns in pursuit of prey. Occasionally takes food from ground, but still in usual style, only pausing briefly before flying back to perch.

☐ **Voice** Call is grating' 'tzee', alarm is 'tzee-tuc', often repeated. Song is a few disjointed, scratchy, notes 'zip-zip-zee-zippi-zee-zee'.

☐ **Nesting** Builds nest of wool, hair and moss, lined with feathers, on ledge, typically against wall of building, supported by climber, or in tree cavity. Lays late May to June; sometimes two broods; four to five green or blue eggs with red-brown speckling; incubation about fourteen days, by female mainly. Young fly after about thirteen days.

☐ **General notes** Can be very unobtrusive, even when nesting close to house. Will use open-fronted nest box, especially fixed to wall behind creeper.

Pied flycatcher *Ficedula hypoleuca*

☐ **Status** Migrant, occurring from April to October. Locally distributed in England, Wales and Scotland; passage only in Ireland. Strongholds in Wales and Welsh borders, and the Lake District, but extending range in Pennine counties and southern uplands of Scotland, reaching the Spey Valley in the north. Outlying population in Devon and Somerset. Passage birds on coast in autumn.

☐ **Habitat** Deciduous woods in hilly places, especially oak, and often near water. Also old orchards and gardens, sometimes in conifers.

☐ **Identification** Quite small; not as large as a sparrow, with more domed head and bull-neck than spotted flycatcher. Male is bold black-and-white, having black-brown head and upperparts; white forehead, underparts, wing-patches and sides of tail. Female is even brown on upperparts; white underparts, wing-patches and sides of tail. Juvenile similar, but duller. Male after post-breeding moult resembles female, but retains white forehead. Bill, eye and legs black. Length 13 cm (5 in).

☐ **Behaviour** Fairly unobtrusive, except when male is singing, both sexes blending well in the light and shade of the tree-canopy where they feed. Diet mainly caterpillars and insects taken from foliage, flies taken on the wing and from the ground. Birds seem to disappear during July, when moult takes place.

☐ **Voice** Call is 'whit'. Song is similar in style to a redstart's: 'zee-it, zee-it' on two notes, sometimes with an occasional trill as well.

☐ **Nesting** Tree hole nester that readily adapts to nest boxes. Nest is made of honeysuckle bark, lined with grasses and hair. Lays mid-May; one brood; five to eight pale blue eggs; incubation about thirteen days, by female only. Fledging occurs about fourteen days later.

☐ **General notes** Every opportunity should be taken to provide nest boxes for this species, not only in gardens but new forestry plantations, too. With encouragement will continue to spread.

Dunnock *Prunella modularis*

☐ **Status** Resident. Distributed widely throughout British Isles except Shetland, where it is found only as an autumn migrant from Continent.

☐ **Habitat** Parks and gardens with cover; hedgerows, scrub and woodland edge.

☐ **Identification** Sparrow sized; superficially similar to female house sparrow but with more streamlined shape and different habits. Grey-brown, crouching bird; upperparts and tail brown with dark streaks; cheek is brown but surrounded by grey which extends down breast to belly; flanks streaked, buffish; dark slender bill; brown eye; pink legs. Sexes similar. Length 14 cm (5½ in).

☐ **Behaviour** Another mouse-like bird, in colouring and temperament, shuffling along on ground or through ground-cover with short hops, searching for insects in spring and summer, and feeding mainly on seeds in autumn and winter. Rarely far from refuge of cover. Flight is low, flitting short distances between cover. Sings pleasant song from higher up in bush.

☐ **Voice** Call is an insistent 'tseep'. Song is like a weak version of wren's: a jingle.

☐ **Nesting** Builds a deep cup of grass and moss, lined with wool and hair, low in hedge or dense conifer, sometimes in brushwood. Lays April to July; two, sometimes three broods; three to five clear turquoise-blue eggs; incubation twelve days, by female only. Fledging takes place after about twelve days also.

☐ **General notes** Not related to sparrows, despite alternative name of hedge-sparrow. Will come to ground feeding station – occasionally bird table – but timid. Frequent host of cuckoo. Will visit for grated cheese and breadcrumbs.

Meadow pipit *Anthus pratensis*

☐ **Status** Resident. Distributed across the British Isles, although not as abundant in parts of central England as elsewhere. Partial migrant.

☐ **Habitat** Moorland, rough grazing, damp meadows, dunes and saltmarsh. Also farmland in winter.

☐ **Identification** Sparrow-sized, streaked bird, rather like a wagtail in shape but with a shorter tail. Upperparts are greeny-brown, streaked with darker brown and black; light buff supercilium and underparts, which are lightly streaked with dark brown; outer tail feathers are white; bill horn; legs pink with very long hind claws. Sexes similar. Length 14 cm (5½ in).

☐ **Behaviour** A ground feeder, walking through long grass or heather with wagtail-like gait, including tail-wagging and sudden lunges after flies. Generally picks up insects, spiders and seeds from ground. On breeding ground rises from ground with characteristic call when flushed, fluttering up in bursts of wing-beats. In winter flocks, birds rise one by one in same way, moving away with rising and falling motion, landing again quite near. Also has 'parachuting' display flight.

□ **Voice** Call is 'tseep', or triple call of same sound. Song is accelerating series of 'chip-chip' and 'swee-swee' notes, ending in a trill as the bird parachutes down to the ground.

□ **Nesting** Builds nest of grass, lined with fine grass or hair, on ground. Lays April to June; two broods; three to five eggs with pale ground of varying colours: mottled, marbled or streaked with darker colours, sometimes plain blue; incubation about fourteen days, by female only. Young leave after further fourteen days.

□ **General notes** Most likely to be encountered in late autumn in country gardens. In 'hard' New Years also in towns, when it will take small items, such as grated cheese and bread crumbs, from ground feeding stations.

Pied wagtail *Motacilla alba*

□ **Status** Resident. Widely distributed throughout the British Isles; scarce in Outer Hebrides and Shetland. Some of our birds migrate in winter.

□ **Habitat** Riversides, lakesides, reservoirs, farmyards and gardens.

□ **Identification** Slim, long-tailed bird, about the size of a sparrow but with slender insect-eater's bill and long, continually wagging tail. Male has black upperparts, with white on sides of tail and on face; double white wing-bar; black throat and breast; white belly. Female similar, but black crown grades into dull grey back. Juvenile is quite yellow, greyish on back, with off-white throat and crescent of dirty black on breast; bill, legs, and eye black. Length 17 cm (6$\frac{1}{2}$ in).

□ **Behaviour** Active bird, rushing after flies on the ground with sudden swerves and lunges, tail wagging. Alternatively may be seen at water's edge, running in bursts, often picking up insects on the waterline. Also catches flies in the air. Often feeds by roads in summer when caterpillars and insects associated with roadside trees are picked off the tarmac. Flight is often quite high, and undulating. Frequently calls in flight. Forms communal roosts in autumn and winter, in reed beds, glasshouses, city centres and at sewage farms.

□ **Voice** Call is 'tchizzik', usually given in flight; also more musical 'tchuwee'. Song is twittering version of call notes.

□ **Nesting** Builds nest of twigs and leaves lined with hair, feathers and wool, in cavity in wall, on a ledge in a building, among creepers or in a hole in a bank. Lays April to June; two or three broods; five or six greyish eggs marked with brown or grey; incubation about fourteen days, by female only. Fledging occurs after a further fourteen days.

□ **General notes** Will use open-fronted nest box or space in stone wall or log pile. Comes to ground feeding station for minute particles of food, such as cheese crumbs, in hard weather.

Grey wagtail *Motacilla cinerea*

□ **Status** Resident. Distributed across the British Isles but local or scarce in eastern lowland England, the Outer Hebrides and Orkneys. Absent from Shetland. Partial migrant.

☐ **Habitat** Prefers faster running water than pied wagtail: rivers, streams and lochans in uplands; usually by mill-races and weirs in lowlands. Slower water, even in towns, in winter.

☐ **Identification** Slightly larger body than pied wagtail; much longer tail. Upperparts, crown and forehead clean grey, tail black with white sides; underparts and rump are bright acid-yellow. Both sexes have white supercilium. Male has moustachial stripe separating grey cheek from black throat; bill black; legs brown. Length 18 cm (7 in).

☐ **Behaviour** Associated more exclusively with water than pied wagtail, feeding on insects at water's edge or from rocks or sand-bars in streams. Perches readily in waterside trees. Can blend well with rushing water when perched on rock in mid-stream, tail bobbing.

☐ **Voice** Call is metallic version of pied wagtail's 'tchizzik'. Twittering song, 'tsee-tee-tee', is seldom heard.

☐ **Nesting** Builds nest of grass and moss, lined with hair in hole in river bank or tree roots, also wall cavities. Lays April to June; sometimes two broods; five buff eggs with grey-brown speckling; incubation about fourteen days, mainly by female. Fledging occurs after about twelve days.

☐ **General notes** Mostly a visitor to streamside gardens in the north and west, when it may nest in a hole in a wall; also watermills in lowlands. More likely than pied wagtail to abandon inland sites for coast in hard weather, when it will take tiny items from ground feeding station.

Starling *Sturnus vulgaris*

☐ **Status** Resident. Widespread across the British Isles; a little scarcer in the west of Ireland. Continental birds winter here.

☐ **Habitat** Town parks, gardens, farmland, moorland edge and grazing marsh.

☐ **Identification** Larger than a sparrow, a little smaller than a thrush; jaunty, active, all-dark bird. Summer plumage is iridescent black, with some buff and white spots, and brown edges to wing feathers; yellow bill. Winter plumage is mattish black with more white speckling; feather edges on wings lighter; bill dull yellow-brown; reddish legs. In flight has compact look, with triangular wings and short tail. Juvenile is grey-brown. Sexes subtly different: female always more spotted and less bright. Length 22 cm (8½ in).

☐ **Behaviour** Noisy, aggressive, garrulous, flocking outside the breeding season. Prefers to feed on short turf, probing the ground with open bill in continuous scissor action, taking all sorts of invertebrate life or feeding among (or on) grazing animals for the flies and ticks associated with them. Flies in dense, whirring flocks, settling noisily at dusk in woods, city centres (on ledges of buildings and trees in squares), or reed beds, to roost.

☐ **Voice** Call is harsh 'tcheer', plus clicking and chuckling noises. Song is a medley of clicks, chuckles, mimicry and trills, usually delivered from a roof top, with wings held drooping and fanned.

☐ **Nesting** Builds untidy grass or straw nest lined with feathers, in tree or cliff hole, under eaves or in roof space. Lays April to May; usually two broods; incubation about fourteen days, by female. Fledging occurs about twenty-one days later.

Starlings are by nature woodland birds in the breeding season, using natural holes in trees as nest sites. Today, however, starlings are much more associated with towns and gardens. They are fascinating to watch, and few other birds allow us such close-up views of their lives. The bird at the bottom is in winter plumage.

Right: *Linnets typically nest in gorse and are generally associated with heaths. They are larger than redpolls and have less streaked plumage. In country areas they visit garden feeding stations to take seeds.*

Right: *Previously uncommon winter visitors to much of England and Wales, siskins began feeding on peanut bags in the 1960s and are now established garden visitors. The spread of conifer plantations has helped them colonize new areas from their strongholds in Scotland, and they now breed in a number of scattered places south of the border.*

Right: *Goldfinches are closely associated with gardens and orchards in the breeding season, when their cheerful tinkling song can be heard.*

Below: *Like the goldfinch, the chaffinch is very much a bird of gardens and orchards, typically singing from a fruit tree in blossom.*

Above: *Eating the buds of fruit trees is behaviour more associated with bullfinches than the greenfinch shown here.*

Left: *Superficially similar to a chaffinch, bramblings have more orange coloured plumage overall. Both sexes have conspicuous white rumps. A winter visitor, only occasionally coming to gardens.*

Left: *The redpoll is a small, streaky, active finch which, like the siskin, has benefited from the planting of new conifer plantations. Also fond of birch and alder seeds.*

Left: *Bullfinches are shy birds, although they may visit large gardens and parks with shrubberies. They are often seen in pairs, when the female's subtler plumage (seen here on the left) can be compared with the rose-pink of the male.*

Above: *The yellowhammer or yellow bunting, and the reed bunting (below), are 'country cousins' of the house sparrow. Both birds are only likely to enter gardens during the winter, although yellowhammers may nes in a suitable boundary hedge.*

♀

♂

Right: *The familiar house sparrow lacks the cheek spot of the neater, chestnut-capped tree sparrow (top right).*

□ **General notes** Keen garden feeder and hole nest box user; needs no encouragement.

Winter sees birds like these starlings forming flocks in order to best exploit available food sources. At dusk these flocks may be observed going to roost.

Greenfinch *Carduelis chloris*

□ **Status** Resident. Occurs throughout the British Isles except Shetland, where it is a rare vagrant.

□ **Habitat** Parks and gardens; tall hedges, farmland and woodland edge.

□ **Identification** Sparrow-sized, green-and-yellow finch with forked tail. Upperparts of male are olive-green, with black wing and tail tips and bright yellow patches on sides of tail and on primary wing feathers; grey patch on wing; underparts are bright greenish-yellow, as is rump when seen in flight. Female is similar but browner, without grey on wings. Bill is heavy and pale; legs pink. Juvenile is like female but softly streaked; bill darker. Female and juvenile can be confused with female house sparrow. Length 15 cm (6 in).

□ **Behaviour** Gregarious outside breeding season, even then tending to nest in loose colonies. Feeding is mainly in trees and bushes, on a wide variety of larger seeds; young fed on smaller seeds and insects. At harvest time grain is taken, the birds rising en masse with whirring wings when disturbed, and moving with bounding flight. Much associated with conifers in breeding season, one often being used as a song post.

□ **Voice** Calls are a trill, 'tsooeet', and during breeding a wheezy 'tsweee'. Flight call is 'chi-chi-chi-chi-chit'. Song is a twittering combination of the call notes, sometimes delivered in fluttering display flight.

□ **Nesting** Builds cup of grass, roots and moss with root lining in a hedge, bush or tree, often an evergreen. Lays April to August; two or three broods; four to six white or pale blue eggs spotted red-brown; incubation about fourteen days, by female only. Fledging occurs about fourteen days later.

□ **General notes** Formerly a farmland bird; now very much a suburban bird. Active and aggressive bird table feeder, especially when there are peanuts or sunflower seeds to be had.

Goldfinch *Carduelis carduelis*

□ **Status** Resident. Widespread across England, Wales and Ireland, scarcer in the north of England and southern Scotland, not breeding north of Inverness. Migratory in northern part of range.

☐ **Habitat** Gardens, parks, orchards, woodland edges, weedy fields and waste ground.

☐ **Identification** Smaller and slighter than sparrow; with unusually fine bill for seed-eater. Upperparts: brown back, black-and-yellow wings; black-and-white tail, with white rump shown in flight; cheeks are white bordered black; crown black; red forehead and throat; underparts pale, with brown on breast grading into white on belly. Sexes similar. Juvenile is streaky, without prominent head markings, but with distinctive wing pattern. Length 13 cm (5 in).

☐ **Behaviour** Gregarious outside breeding season, forming small parties rather than flocks. Feeds on seeds of thistle, burdock, teazel, etc. taking the seed out of the dead flower with much fluttering and twittering. Young are fed mainly on insects. Flight is undulating, with flight calls.

☐ **Voice** Call is tinkling 'tswit-wit-wit'. Song is twittering, liquid extended version.

☐ **Nesting** Builds neat cup of moss and lichen, lined with wool and down, in tree or tall hedge, often near end of branch. Lays May to August; two or three broods; five to six light blue eggs with brown spots; incubation about twelve days, by female. Fledging occurs after about fourteen days.

☐ **General notes** Much associated with waste ground in towns, and with orchard trees. Near extinct at the turn of the century due to bird-catching and increased cultivation; nowadays less associated with farmland. Regular garden nester, and casual bird table user for seeds and nuts.

Siskin *Carduelis spinus*

☐ **Status** Resident. Breeding mainly in Scotland and Ireland, with scattered locations in England and Wales associated with great conifer forests. Disperses widely in winter.

☐ **Habitat** Coniferous and mixed woods during breeding season; also areas of birch and alder in winter, and gardens.

☐ **Identification** Smaller than a sparrow; miniature finch with deeply forked tail; active and agile. Upperparts of male are olive-green streaked black; yellow double wing-bar; yellow on sides of tail and rump; head, nape and breast are yellow; crown and patch on throat black; rest of underparts grade into white, streaked with black. Female is similar but duller overall, with streaky head lacking black cap and bib of male. Juvenile is duller and streakier than female. Black and yellow areas noticeable in flight. Bill yellowish-grey; legs pink. Length 12 cm (4½ in).

☐ **Behaviour** Feeds actively in trees; mainly on spruce and pine seeds during breeding season, birch seeds in autumn, alder in winter, when often found in waterside groups of trees. Young also fed on insects. Fairly quiet when feeding, but flying birds make frequent contact calls. Bounding flight, moving quickly in groups from one tree to another. May be quite unafraid when feeding low down on outer branches of tree, frequently tit-like, hanging upside-down and using feet to hold cones.

☐ **Voice** Call, often in flight, is liquid 'tsu', also wheezy 'tsu-eet'. Song is twittering with trills and warbles and greenfinch-like wheezes, one of which terminates the song. Also has butterfly-like song flight.

Red nutbags have a particular appeal for siskins.

□ **Nesting** Builds small, neat cup of moss, lichens and grass, lined with down, high in conifer. Lays April to June; usually two broods; three to five pale blue eggs with purplish markings; incubation about twelve days, by female only. Fledging occurs after about fourteen days.

□ **General notes** Increasing as winter visitor to gardens, especially for peanuts. Also drinks frequently.

Linnet *Carduelis cannabina*

□ **Status** Resident. Widespread across the British Isles except Hebrides and Orkney and Shetland. Less common in north-west Scotland. Southward movement occurs in winter.

□ **Habitat** Heath and commons with gorse, scrub and gardens. Weedy fields, saltmarsh and rough grazing in winter.

□ **Identification** Slightly smaller than sparrow; slim buff-and-brown finch associated with gorse in breeding season. Upperparts mainly unmarked chestnut-brown, with blackish outer wing with white feather edges; white outer tail feathers; dark tip to forked tail; head grey (male has red forehead and breast in breeding season, faded in winter); female and male have streaked throat, female has brown streaks on light buff underparts; male paler and unstreaked below. Length 13 cm (5 in).

□ **Behaviour** Vocal, flocking bird, feeding on weed seeds with typical 'head bent down' pose, or on ground with sparrows, yellowhammers and other finches. Bouncy, erratic flight, with impression of white in wings and tail. Takes insects during breeding season, when characteristically perches on gorse to deliver song.

□ **Voice** Call is 'tsooeet'; in flight rapid 'chi-chi-chi-chit'. Song is musical twitter, with twangy notes.

□ **Nesting** Builds grass and moss nest lined with hair and wool near ground in bush. Lays April to July; two or three broods; four to six bluish-white eggs with a few purple-red blotches; incubation about eleven days, mainly by female. Fledging occurs after about twelve days.

□ **General notes** Occasionally nests in boundary hedges or shrubberies. Will take seeds, etc. from bird table.

Redpoll *Acanthis flammea*

□ **Status** Resident. Widespread in Ireland and Scotland, although absent from islands and extreme north of Scotland; common in north and central Wales, but scarcer in the south and absent from extreme south-west. In England most common in north-west; absent from upper Thames valley and Cornwall. Still expanding its range. Southward movement occurs in winter.

□ **Habitat** Mainly conifer plantations on heaths and moors; also birch and alder woods, large gardens and shrubberies..

□ **Identification** Small streaky finch with forked tail; flocking outside breeding season. Upperparts of both sexes brown with variable black streaking and white feather edging; whitish double wing-bars. Male has red on forehead and pinkish rump; pink flush on breast in late winter/spring; rest of underparts pale, streaked on flanks. Female has less red on crown. Both sexes have black bib; bill yellowish; legs dark. Juvenile has no red in plumage. Length 12 cm (4½ in).

☐ **Behaviour** Similar to siskin, with which it associates in winter. More likely than siskin to be seen feeding on plants, occasionally on ground for seeds; eats insects in spring. Typical bounding flight of small finches; distinctive flight call.

☐ **Voice** Flight call is trill 'rrr' followed by 'chee-chee-chee' or with an extra note 'chu-chu-chu-chu'; also 'tiu' and nasal 'twee'. Song is combination of calls with trills.

☐ **Nesting** Flimsy twig cup lined with down, often low in bush or tree. Lays May to June; sometimes two broods; four to six light blue eggs with pale brown spots and streaks; incubation about eleven days, by female only. Fledging occurs about twelve days later.

☐ **General notes** Takes seeds from bird table. More likely to come to garden with birch, alder or conifer trees.

Bullfinch *Pyrrhula pyrrhula*

☐ **Status** Resident. Widely distributed across British Isles except extreme north and west; absent from Isle of Man and Scottish islands.

☐ **Habitat** Woods, orchards, gardens, scrubby thickets and overgrown hedgerows.

☐ **Identification** Sparrow-sized, thickset finch; shy. Male has grey back; black cap; tail and wings have white wing-bar; white rump shows in flight; cheek, breast and belly rose-pink; lower underparts white. Female is like dull male, with grey-brown back and brownish-pink underparts. Juvenile browner than female; lacks black cap. Length 15 cm (6 in).

☐ **Behaviour** Quiet and retiring. Often seen in pairs, usually in cover, feeding on seeds, especially ash 'keys', buds and blossom in spring, and weeds seeds and berries in autumn. Young also fed caterpillars. Will feed on ground with other finches in crop fields in winter, but likes cover nearby. Flight is undulating, usually low between bushes.

☐ **Voice** Low, soft call, a whistled 'wheeb' or deeu'. Song is no louder than a subsong, consisting of creaky warbles.

☐ **Nesting** Builds cup of twigs, moss and lichen, lined with roots and hair, in bramble, thick hedge or evergreen. Lays April to July; two or three broods; four or five green-blue eggs with purple-brown streaks and spots; incubation about fourteen days, mainly by female. Fledging occurs about fourteen days later.

☐ **General notes** Comes to gardens for natural foods, peanuts and some seeds in winter, but shy temperament makes it unsuitable for bird tables.

Bullfinches take the seeds from blackberries long after the flesh has become inedible.

Crossbill *Loxia curvirostra*

☐ **Status** Resident, but moving freely outside breeding season. May irrupt in late summer. Breeds mainly in Scotland, New Forest, Breckland and Keilder Forest.

☐ **Habitat** Conifer plantations, especially spruce. Scottish crossbill (separate race) found in old Caledonian pine stands.

☐ **Identification** Larger than chaffinch; bulky. Mature males brick red; young males dull red. Females dull grey-green with yellower rump. Juveniles like streaky females, but crossed bill not so pronounced as in adult. Scottish birds have heavier bill. Length 16 cm (6¼ in).

☐ **Behaviour** Parrot-like, clambering around tops of conifers in small parties, cutting off cones with beak, holding them with foot and tearing them open for seeds inside. Flight undulating. Drinks frequently. Behaviour tame.

☐ **Voice** Call is like the chirping of a sparrow, only deeper, 'chip-chip-chip'. Often given in flight. Song resembles that of a greenfinch, but more varied and without the wheezing notes.

☐ **Nesting** Nest of twigs lined with grass high in conifer. Lays February to March; one brood; three to four eggs, green with purple-red marks at blunt end; incubation fourteen days, by female only. Young fledge after eighteen days.

☐ **General notes** May be seen at all times near breeding site, usually when coming to drink. Away from breeding site seen in late summer or winter, especially if spruce or pine are nearby. May nest in garden conifers if close to forest. Drinks often, but may only be at water for a few seconds each time.

Chaffinch *Fringilla coelebs*

☐ **Status** Resident. Widespread and common across the British Isles except Shetland, where it occurs rarely. Large numbers of Continental birds winter here.

☐ **Habitat** Parks and gardens, woodland, hedgerows, farmland.

☐ **Identification** A fraction larger than a sparrow; cheerful pink and grey finch (male); female rather like female house sparrow. Male is quite striking; with grey crown (slightly crested) and nape contrasting with pink cheeks, breast and upper belly, grading into white; prominent white shoulder-patch, wing-bars and outer tail feathers all show in flight, as does greenish rump; back is pinkish-brown. Female is much more subdued, generally greenish-brown above; paler below; same wing and tail patterns as male. Bill is grey in male, brown in female; legs pinkish-brown. Length 15 cm (6 in).

☐ **Behaviour** Has typically jerky walking action on ground, and a lighter hop than sparrows. Feeds on all sorts of vegetable and animal matter, searching leaf litter in woods in winter or feeding in flocks in fields in spring; investigates tree foliage for caterpillars which it feeds to young. Undulating flight with wings closed every few beats. Often tame in parks and gardens when fed.

☐ **Voice** Call is 'pink-pink'; also 'wheet' in spring; in flight 'chip'. Song has recognizable pattern with many local variations: 'chip-chip-chip-chuwee-chuwee-tissi-chooeeo', finishing with a flourish.

☐ **Nesting** Builds neat cup of moss and lichen with wool, hair and feather lining, in tree-fork, hedge or bush. Lays April to June; one or two broods; three to six buff eggs with purple-brown blotches; incubation about fourteen days, by female only. Fledging occurs after about twelve days.

☐ **General notes** Formerly regarded as our most abundant bird, now less common. Nests and feeds in gardens, making good use of bird table for all sorts of scraps as well as seeds, berries, etc.

Brambling *Fringilla montifringilla*

☐ **Status** Migrant, occurring from October to April. Occurs widely across British Isles except in north-west Scotland (although it has bred occasionally here), more numerous in eastern England, Wales and Ireland.

☐ **Habitat** Near beech trees, stubble and weedy crop fields; gardens in hard weather.

☐ **Identification** Sparrow sized; shape like chaffinch but shorter, with forked tail. Winter male has mottled brown upperparts and black wings with pale feather edges; black tail; white rump and wing-bars; light orange breast extends to shoulders; rest of underparts white, grey speckling on flanks. Females similar but duller. Summer male has all-black head and back, with black bill. Winter bills of both sexes are yellow with dark tip; legs pink/straw. Juvenile as female. Length 15 cm (6 in).

☐ **Behaviour** Flocking species, much associated with beech trees, feeding on ground among fallen leaves; well camouflaged. Whole group will fly up when disturbed to perch in nearby tree or hedge, returning to ground one by one when danger is over. Eats beech mast, weed seeds, berries, grain, and insects in spring. Flight similar to that of chaffinch; slightly erratic.

☐ **Voice** Likely to be fairly silent during winter except for chaffinch-like flight call, or grating 'tsweek'. Late departing birds in spring may wheeze like greenfinch. Song is a few sweet and melodious flute-like notes.

☐ **Nesting** *Very* rare breeder in Scotland. Builds deep cup of grass and moss, lined with feathers and decorated with bark and lichens, in a tree, usually a birch or conifer. Lays mid-May in south of range; one brood; six to seven clouded-green eggs, with red-brown spots; incubation about fourteen days, by female. Fledging also takes about fourteen days.

☐ **General notes** Wintering areas dependent on beech-mast crop, so may appear in large numbers one year then miss several. Takes seed at ground feeders.

Yellowhammer *Emberiza citrinella*

☐ **Status** Resident. Widespread across British Isles except Hebrides, Shetland and some moorlands in northern Scotland where it is rare.

☐ **Habitat** Farmland hedgerows, scrub, upland conifer plantations (young), bracken; stubble fields and stack-yards in winter.

☐ **Identification** Bigger than a sparrow, with long tail; fairly slim body; head small by proportion. Male has striking yellow head and underparts, with dark streaks on head; chestnut on sides of breast and flanks; back is chestnut, with buff and black streaks; chestnut rump and white outer feathers to black tail. Female duller, although retains chestnut rump.

Juvenile buff and brown; chestnut rump; bill horn; legs pink/straw. Length 17 cm (6½ in).

☐ **Behaviour** Feeds mainly on the ground, moving with short hops, picking up grain and seed; also insects and invertebrates. Flocks in winter. Flight is similar to finches but jerky. Kinks tail on landing, revealing white feathers. Male usually sings from isolated bush or tall part of hedgerow.

☐ **Voice** Song is well known as 'little-bit-of-bread-and-no-cheese'. Calls are 'chip' and 'twit-up'.

☐ **Nesting** Builds grass nest lined with hair low down in hedge or on ground. Lays April to August; two or three broods; two to five white or pinky-white eggs, with dark scribbling; incubation about fourteen days, by female only. Fledging takes about twelve days.

☐ **General notes** May nest in boundary hedge of country garden, and visit bird table or ground feeder in hard weather for grain, seeds, etc.

Reed bunting *Emberiza schoeniclus*

☐ **Status** Resident. Widely distributed across the British Isles. Some Continental birds winter here.

☐ **Habitat** Reed beds, rushy fields, water margins; increasingly drier areas like chalk downs, scrub and allotments. Stubble and crop fields in winter.

☐ **Identification** A little bigger than a sparrow, with which it may be confused; has bunting shape, however. Male in summer has black head, throat and breast, with thin white moustache stripe linking white collar and underparts; flanks streaked brown; back chestnut streaked with black; white outer tail feathers, black inner feathers. In winter black parts of plumage much paler; in late summer/autumn black parts reduced to greyish cap and cheek. Female lacks black head of male, but has larger moustache stripe; underparts well-streaked. Stout dark bill, darkish legs. Juvenile similar to female. Length 15 cm (6 in).

☐ **Behaviour** Frequently flicks tail and wings when perched. Hops on ground, looking for seeds, etc. and some animal food. Also creeps dunnock-like or runs on ground. Flocks in fields with other finches and buntings in winter. Flight is flitting, usually going low into cover. Sings from prominent perch.

☐ **Voice** Call is 'seeu' or 'seep'. Song is monotonous 'zip-zip-zip-chitikk'.

☐ **Nesting** Grass cup lined with fine grass or hair placed at base of reeds or in tussock. Lays April to June; two or three broods; three to five eggs with variable background: olive, blue or pale green, with black marks; incubation about fourteen days, mainly by female. Fledging takes about twelve days.

☐ **General notes** Will enter gardens in hard weather for grain, seeds, etc.

House sparrow *Passer domesticus*

☐ **Status** Resident. Widespread and common across the British Isles.

☐ **Habitat** Close to human habitation in town and country. Flocks in fields in winter.

☐ **Identification** Familiar jaunty, fearless bird; has seed-eater's stubby bill; fairly dumpy body; shortish wings and tail. Male has chestnut back and wings with black streaks and pale feather edges; grey rump extends well up back; brown tail; back of crown and nape are chestnut; rest of crown and forehead grey; lores and 'bib' black; cheek and underparts are unmarked grey; in poor light male house sparrows can look remarkably grey all over; black bill: bill is paler in winter; bib rather mottled; head pattern less distinct. Female has chestnut upperparts, streaked with buff and black; underparts browny-grey; pale cheek and supercilium; bill horn. Legs of both sexes pink. Juvenile like female. Length 15 cm (6 in).

☐ **Behaviour** Gregarious, pugnacious and bold. Tame where fed. Feeds on ground, moving with rather heavy footed hops. Takes grain, seeds, scraps of vegetable and animal matter, insects, etc. Opportunist feeder. Perches in noisy groups on gutters, in trees and on lawns. Forms communal roosts in winter. Also one of few species to use nest site as roost. Flight is straight with whirring wings; more bouncy over longer distances.

☐ **Voice** Has variety of calls: 'chirp', 'cheep', and often 'chissik'. Song is medley of calls, usually delivered from roof top or gutter.

☐ **Nesting** Builds untidy dome of straw, grass, bits of paper, etc., lined with feathers under eaves, in hole in building, tree, nest box or in hedge. Lays April to August; two or three broods; three to five white eggs, with brown and grey blotches; incubation about fourteen days, mainly by female. Fledging occurs after about fourteen days.

☐ **General notes** Needs no encouragement at bird table or feeder, where it has learnt to cling to peanut bags, etc. Worth watching for social behaviour and ease with which it can be observed.

Tree sparrow *Passer montanus*

☐ **Status** Resident. Patchy distribution; commoner in east, absent from most of the West Country, parts of west Wales, the high Pennines and Lake District Fells, higher parts of the Scottish uplands and west coast and most of inland Ireland. Rare in Orkney and Shetland.

☐ **Habitat** Cultivated land and parkland with old trees, ruins, etc. affording nest sites. Stubble fields, etc. in winter.

☐ **Identification** A little smaller than house sparrow; cleaner, neater appearance. Plumage very much like male house sparrow's but lacks grey on head and rump; underparts are buffer; upperparts less red; crown is rich chestnut; black 'bib' neater and more compact; pale grey cheek almost forms collar; has black spot on cheek; bill is black; legs pink. Sexes similar. Length 14 cm (5½ in).

☐ **Behaviour** Shyer and quieter than house sparrow; a country bird, associated with trees in breeding season. Feeds on ground on seeds, grain and insects. Flight as house sparrow. Chirruping is more musical than house sparrow's.

☐ **Voice** Calls similar to a house sparrow's: 'chip-chip', 'chop' and 'chit-tchup'. Flight call is 'teck'. Song is a medley of calls.

☐ **Nesting** Breeds in loose colonies, building straw and grass nest in hole in tree, wall or cliff; sometimes nest box. Lays April to July; two or three broods; three to five white eggs, blotched with brown; incubation about eleven days, by both parents. Fledging occurs after about fourteen days.

☐ **General notes** May nest in country gardens. Shy bird table visitor, taking seeds, grain, scraps, etc. Also feeds at pheasant grain hoppers.

Unusual visitors

Of the seventy main species covered in this book, about half are only occasional, if regular, visitors to gardens. In addition, the visiting pattern of a single species may vary throughout the country. For instance in the West Country, the appearance of a tree sparrow would cause a stir, in the south-east, a pied flycatcher would make a red-letter day, while a goldfinch feeding on a thistle in the north of Scotland would be noteworthy.

Many of our migratory birds appear mainly in gardens on passage, like garden warblers and whitethroats, or are driven into gardens by hunger, like bramblings. Shy woodland birds such as nuthatches, willow tits and redstarts are consistent but infrequent visitors, although certain individuals may come regularly to a favoured spot, and all have bred in gardens. Flocking birds, like yellowhammers and meadow pipits, rarely enter gardens until the ground is frozen solid, following the chaffinches or greenfinches which enter gardens more readily to find food put out for them. Then there are the drinkers such as crossbills and hawfinches whose seed diet forces them to take water frequently, which will drop down to a garden pond, take two or three sips of water, and slip back to the tree tops. Finally there are the new colonists, birds necessarily rare because of their recent arrival to our shores, but capable of rapid expansion if conditions are right. Who could have foreseen in 1955 that an isolated breeding record of a pair of collared doves in Norfolk would herald an invasion that covered the British Isles in fifteen years?

In a restricted area in the south of England, serins have launched a spearhead invasion, based mainly on birds nesting in gardens that most resemble their Mediterranean origins. Like the collared dove, these little yellow finches, with their cheerful tinkling song, have undergone an expansionist stage in their development, spreading north through France to the English Channel. The first birds bred here in 1967, but although they seem established at their beachhead, they have not made much progress in recent years. Firecrests, slightly larger and brighter than goldcrests and with a prominent eye-stripe, were regular passage visitors to Britain, appearing most frequently in gardens in late autumn. Now established at a number of sites in the south of England as breeding birds, their appearance is to be expected at any time of the year.

A ring-necked parakeet – an escaped species now thriving in areas where it is fed.

PASSAGE VISITORS

Most of our unusual visitors turn up on passage – birds which arrive in spring being overshoots from southern Europe. Of these, the hoopoe is the best known, seemingly having a penchant for vicarage lawns. It probably occurs as often on broken ground more closely resembling its olive-grove haunts around the Mediterranean, but doubtless shows up better against a verdant green background! Very occasionally it breeds, and naturalist Tony Soper cites the case of a pair that used a hole in a cob wall in Hampshire, whose fledgling fell out of the nest. It was put into an open bird cage that was hung from the wall, and was fed successfully there by the parents.

The golden oriole, another impressive-looking visitor from the south, also turns up occasionally on spring migration, usually near the coast. Abroad, it nests in gardens as well as parks and woods, and in Britain might enter a garden with tall trees. The bird would certainly pass unnoticed except for its fluty song, usually rendered as 'weela-weeo', because it keeps to the tree canopy, where even the striking black-and-yellow plumage of the male blends with the dappled shade.

Autumn passage brings the greatest variety of species, and east coast gardens can be teeming with passerines after a 'fall'. These tend to happen when birds that normally pass over East Anglia en route from Scandinavia experience misty conditions over the North Sea and land near the coast until conditions improve. This phenomenon occurs right up the east coast as far north as Shetland, when they are more likely to be associated with strong south-easterly winds that drift the birds from their intended course. As well as the commoner species (like pied flycatchers) bluethroats, red-breasted flycatchers, wrynecks, red-backed shrikes and barred warblers are sometimes the victims of weather conditions. These last three have a habit of turning up together, so if you find one, look for the others! Many of these birds will be exhausted, and will allow a close approach, but it is our responsibility not to harass them in our eagerness to have a close look. Left in peace they will feed quietly, allowing plenty of opportunity for close observation.

WRECKS AND VAGRANTS

A similar occurrence to the 'fall' is a 'wreck', which is more likely on the western side of Britain. This happens when very strong winds blow seabirds way off-course, when they may turn up anywhere, exhausted and disorientated. Typical of a 'wreck' was the gannet found in a car park in Cambridgeshire, or the little auk in a garden in Devon. If you do find a seabird in your garden, feed it some cat-food or sprats, keep it in a box in a quiet place, and try to get it to the sea as soon as it has recovered its strength. Don't worry about trying to get your seabird back on to a sea cliff, because at this time of the year your bird is a deep sea dweller, and the beach at Skegness will do just as well as the cliffs on Anglesey!

Weather conditions are the usual reason for vagrancy, but there are other causes. After fledging, juvenile birds of many species move away from the natal area in a random direction known as 'post-breeding dispersal'. Migratory birds may not adopt their instinctive route until they have travelled considerable distances, and may appear in gardens in search of food. Birds bred in Britain, like whitethroats, or Continental species, like the barred warbler, may be accounted for in this way.

Migrants from Siberia and other parts of Asia are explained by a different theory. Long-distance migrants frequently use a 'great circle' route, following the curvature of the earth to take them the shortest distance to their destination. For reasons we do not fully understand, birds like Pallas's warbler, which breed in Asian USSR, sometimes take a reverse migration, which takes them to western Europe instead of south-east Asia. What happens to these birds after they have left our shores we do not know, because unfortunately no feasible tracking system exists, but if they hold their course and continue their migration they would end up south of the equator.

Some notable rarities have been recorded in gardens, particularly when they lie close to established landfalls, like Fair Isle, the Scillies, and north Norfolk. The attraction of gardens is that they may be the first piece of cover that the migrant can find after arriving on a windswept beach or headland, and birds like rose-coloured starlings, Isabelline shrikes, bluethroats and rollers have all turned up in gardens. You could even have a first for Britain, like the myrtle warbler from America that was discovered feeding on marmalade on a bird table in Devon!

Perhaps the best-known and most watched garden rarity of recent years was the celebrated olive-backed pipit in Bracknell, Berkshire. This American vagrant appeared in late winter 1983/4, coming regularly to a private garden where food was put out for the birds by a dedicated birdwatcher. After a few days had passed, the owner of the garden announced the news, making it clear that he and his wife were prepared to let other birdwatchers see the bird under controlled conditions. This they did, in their thousands, being invited into the lounge to watch the bird, sometimes being offered a cup of tea, and usually leaving a donation in thanks for the kindness shown.

IRRUPTIONS

Another feature of bird migration is the irruption, an irregular movement of large numbers of birds from their usual wintering area, triggered off by a shortage of food. Most irruptive species come from the taiga, the great forest belt which stretches across the northerly temperate zone of the

Gale force winds sometimes blow seabirds, like this little auk, way off-course, 'wrecking' them in the most unlikely places.

world. These birds are specialized feeders, and the failure of one particular crop of natural fruit means the birds have to move en masse. The most likely to be found in gardens is the waxwing, which depends heavily on the fruit of the rowan. In irruption years small parties of waxwings may turn up anywhere, frequently coming to gardens for the berries of ornamental shrubs, and occasionally visiting the bird table.

Crossbills are another irruptive species, and most of the birds breeding in Britain are derived from irrupting birds that stayed on through the breeding season. Their preferred food is spruce seeds, which are extracted from the cone with the formidable crossed beak, and in years of shortage pine, fir and larch seeds become substitutes. This exclusively seed diet is extremely dry, and crossbills make frequent visits to water to drink. In wet weather they may find adequate water in puddles in the ruts of forest rides, but dry weather may see them making repeated visits to garden ponds to quench their thirst.

Nutcrackers, crow-like birds from the forests of Siberia, are less predictable in their arrival. In the winter of 1969, when the last great irruption took place, nutcrackers were observed to feed on fat and bread at garden feeding stations. Other individuals, looking for substitutes for the seeds of the arolla pine, took to killing and eating sparrows! In the autumn of 1983, there was a great immigration of jays to our shores from the Continent. This was probably due to a shortage of acorns in Europe, as jays store large numbers of these nuts to carry them over the winter period. Great spotted woodpeckers, which feed largely on conifer seeds during winter in the north of their range, also irrupt occasionally, as may coal, great and blue tits.

Still unusual in winter, though increasing each year, are records of over-wintering chiffchaffs and blackcaps, which visit bird tables, particularly in the New Year. These birds appear to come from Scandinavia, seeking out the milder parts of Britain, but occurring as far north as the west of Scotland. This overwintering habit may well have developed with the aid of garden feeding – fat, bread and fruit all proving popular food. At the bird table blackcaps have revealed themselves as quite aggressive, refusing to give way to starlings and blackbirds, and dominating other aggressive species like great tits.

The mobility of birds is one of their fascinations, bringing an element of chance to the pastime that can hardly be equalled. I well remember seeing my first bittern, springing up out of a tiny patch of reeds beside a polluted stream, then drifting away to the cover of the overgrown sewage farm nearby. It was a completely overwhelming experience, and all the more enjoyable for being within a kilometre or so of home, in the suburbs of Surrey! The patient observer in the garden may well be rewarded in the same way, especially if they are aware of the weather conditions that are likely to increase the chance of a rarity.

If you do discover a rarity, take a full description of it, and let your county recorder know. Our knowledge of birds, and the subsequent opportunity to aid them, is only as good as the combined observations of amateur birdwatchers, to whom the professionals will always be indebted.

Uninvited guests

Any garden, however barren, will have its surprise visitors. Insects, birds and some of the smaller mammals can be very mobile, and may turn up in the most unlikely places if just passing through.

As I have stressed elsewhere, the healthy garden has a full range of plant and animal species co-existing in a balance of sorts, and it may only be our bias towards songbirds, or even a particular type of plant, that puts a certain species beyond the pale. Any distinction between welcome and unwelcome visitors to the garden is bound to be subjective, but for the purpose of this chapter my criterion is based upon whether the creature is specifically harmful to birds in particular and garden life in general; if it is not, it will be considered welcome.

WELCOME GUESTS

Many of the favoured species have been touched upon already; the beautiful and harmless butterflies, to which it is difficult to imagine anyone objecting (although not everyone may be so well disposed towards some of their caterpillars), dragonflies, grass snakes and frogs. But what of the other major group of non-avian visitors, namely the mammals?

MAMMALS

Depending in which part of the country you live, and its surroundings,

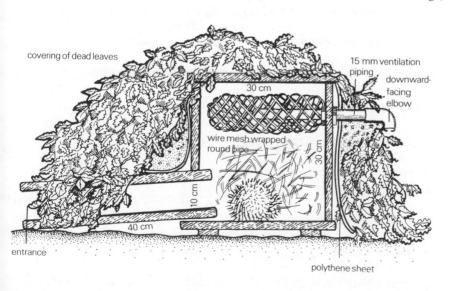

Section through a hedgehog hutch of the type devised by the Henry Doubleday Research Association.

covering of dead leaves

15 mm ventilation piping

downward-facing elbow

30 cm

wire mesh wrapped round pipe

30 cm

10 cm

40 cm

entrance

polythene sheet

virtually any mammal resident in Britain may enter a garden at some time, usually in the dead of night. Certain species are more familiar than others, however, and of these the hedgehog is probably the most popular. Evidence of a visit by a hedgehog is usually found on the ground first thing in the morning; a couple of jet-black droppings, each about the size of a large garden slug – which is probably what the hedgehog has been eating. Put out some milk for it at dusk, and if you have no suitable cover in which it can hide during the day, you could provide a hedgehog kennel. If hedgehogs don't come into your garden, but could find food and shelter there, why not introduce one found near a road? Early spring to mid May, August, and from mid-October to December are ideal times to do this. Outside these times you risk separating a female from her litter or an individual from its chosen place of hibernation.

Foxes are frequent nocturnal visitors to gardens, especially in towns, where they will probably be intent on investigating your dustbin. This can be a nuisance, and you would be advised to keep your bin out of reach in a garage or shed. Foxes are by no means only interested in meat, however, being particularly fond of fallen fruit. They are little threat to garden birds, and watching one at night loping about intent on finding food is a rare thrill, so unaccustomed are we to watching mammals in the wild.

With many mammals there is little we can do to attract them, so much depending on location. If your garden borders woodland, you may be visited by deer, and they will no doubt be very welcome if they restrict themselves to grazing your lawn. The same is true of rabbits, but both are capable of inflicting considerable damage to garden crops and trees. Young trees can be protected by fencing around them for the first ten years or so, but the only answer to crop damage is total deer or rabbit-proof fencing. This may also exclude badgers, which do occasionally visit woodside gardens, even having setts in a few large gardens with suitable terrain. Like foxes, they will eat practically anything, and the only wild birds that really need fear them are the ground nesters.

Mice, voles and shrews may come if there is plenty of ground cover, ample food and nooks and crannies where they can nest, and their predators may follow. Some people place a piece of corrugated iron in the garden to make homes for them, leaving it to become overgrown. Toads, lizards and slow worms may also take advantage of this, and any large stone or rotting piece of wood with a slight depression under it will soon become home to some creature, usually a beetle or centipede, that will feed a bird or even a reptile, but occasionally one of the larger and more endearing mammals.

Finally, a word in favour of bats and moles. Bats are quite harmless, and are under great threat because of current building and wood-treatment practices. In fact, bats are protected by law. If you have them, cherish them. If you don't have them and wish to encourage them you may be prepared to create access into a roof space for them (they can enter through a ventilation louvre), or can build a bat nest box. Moles can be a downright nuisance to a perfectly kept lawn, but the average lawn can take it. Rake the mole hill out over the grass, filling in the hole at the same time, and water. I defy you to notice any difference to your lawn from a few metres away!

POND LIFE

Unlike most mammals, which will decide for themselves whether or not

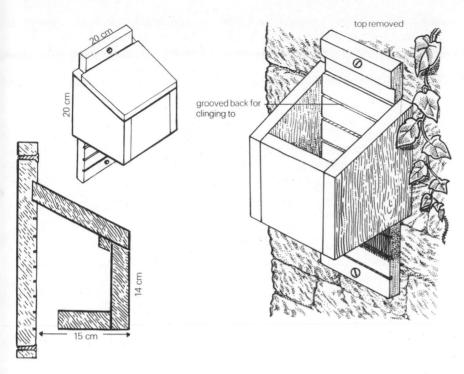

20 cm

20 cm

top removed

grooved back for
clinging to

14 cm

15 cm

*With sites for roosting
and breeding at a
premium, bats need all
the help they can get.*

to come into your garden, all sorts of life may be introduced to a garden pond, although it is surprising what will turn up of its own accord. If you are stocking with spawn or native fishes, do try to obtain these from someone else's pond, so that you don't deplete the hard-pressed natural stock elsewhere. Recommended stocking for fishes is one individual per 90 cm² (14 sq in), for water snails it is two individuals for the same area. Introduced tadpoles may not flourish unless there is some iodine in the water, so derive your pond water from a pond that successfully rears tadpoles.

INSECTS

Insects, many of which start their lives in water, are the other free colonists of the garden. Many are beneficial, pollinating the flowers as they travel from plant to plant in search of nectar. A certain number of foliage-eaters should be tolerated, too, either because they turn into something useful later, like a moth, or because they provide natural food for birds, frogs and toads. As well as this natural control, many plants can be protected from insect and fungal attack by interplanting, which was no doubt why the cottage garden habitually mixed vegetables with the flowers in the border. This may not be as daft as it sounds, because in a monoculture a pest can move freely from one plant to the next, and destroy the lot with ease. Interplanting will also work because many herbivores find their food by scent, and if the scent of (say) a lettuce is overpowered by that of a tobacco plant, the lettuce-eating grub will never reach its destination. The third benefit is in attracting the predators of pests, so that planting shrubby cinquefoil under roses will attract hoverflies, whose larvae feed on aphids. Other recommended mixtures are: basil and French marigolds with tomatoes; tomatoes with brassicas; marigolds, asters and black-eyed susans with cabbages and beans; mint with beans and carrots with onions. Elswhere, song thrushes eat snails, toads eat slugs while centipedes eat their eggs, hedgehogs eat the potato-loving millipedes, and lacewing larvae and ladybirds eat aphids (greenfly and blackfly). If your beans or elders get blackfly, pinch out the infested tips complete with blackfly and the plant will fork at this spot and carry on regardless.

UNWELCOME GUESTS

From time to time your garden will attract some form of wildlife whose habits, in the confines of the garden, are not to be tolerated.

BIRDS

The following birds may be regarded as unwelcome visitors at some time, although they are only behaving as their instincts tell them to. Magpies have already been discussed at length, and the same applies to carrion crows, jackdaws and jays, all inveterate nest raiders – although I think most people would be delighted to see such a colourful bird as a jay at their bird table in the middle of winter. Starlings are regarded as a nuisance by many and, like crows, go to roost fairly early, so you may avoid them by putting food out later in the afternoon when you've noticed the starlings heading to roost. Sparrowhawks and kestrels may visit bird tables to prey on the small birds that visit them, and kestrels often adopt sparrowhawk tactics in towns, catching house sparrows by surprising them from behind a building. Neither is to be deplored, and I would be pleased to see either visit my garden occasionally. Some protection can be offered by having a roof over the bird table, or using one of the other enclosed designs described in the chapter on Feeding garden birds.

If you have a pond, you may be visited by a heron or kingfisher, eager to do a spot of fishing. If you really can't sustain the loss, there are a number

Whereas a kingfisher can be deterred by stocking larger fish, a heron may wipe out your fish population in a matter of days unless you stock with very large specimens or take measures such as those shown here or described in the text. The 'easy pickings' seen in the top illustration can be reduced by positioning a small fence around the pond or reducing the water level so that the heron cannot reach its prey.

Two uncommon garden visitors. A brick-red male crossbill (left) is a good deal more noticeable than the green female. In most years only a few waxwings (below) visit this country, but every so often an 'invasion' occurs. In these years they are likely to be found in gardens as anywhere else, as they depend heavily on the berries of ornamental shrubs.

Right: *A hoopoe –*
culture shock for man
and bird! Against a
broken background this
bird is remarkably well
camouflaged.

Right: *Late summer may*
bring a young cuckoo to
the garden. The brown
plumage will help it hide
from predators, but it
will probably be mobbed
by the ever-watchful
songbirds.

Left: *Pheasants are not unusual on waste ground in towns, and may also raid the garden vegetable patch. Hard weather may make them even more likely to occur.*

Below: *Hawfinches may drop down to take a few sips of water from a garden pond, before returning to the safety of the trees.*

Left: *An urban bird, but with an average of only about thirty pairs breeding annually, black redstarts are more likely to turn up in gardens near the coast during migration.*

Above: *Probably our most familiar mammal in any reasonably wooded district, the grey squirrel can be a pest in gardens, taking all the food from feeders and bird tables in a very short space of time.*

Right: *Hedgehogs were formerly kept by vegetable gardeners for their value in controlling garden pests, and are still welcome visitors to all kinds of gardens today.*

Right: *Badgers occasionally make their homes in larger gardens. Even those which do not nest in gardens may still come from outlying areas to forage.*

of deterrents you could try. One way round the problem is to stock with fishes that are too large for either to cope with, anything much over stickleback size in the case of a kingfisher, whereas a heron will not take anything over the size of a carp. You could place a net over the pond, although this would be less pleasing to look at and would reduce its value for other wildlife. A steep, high side to the pond will make it difficult for a heron to fish, but this may trap animals in the pond, and will make it awkward for birds to bathe. Another deterrent for herons is to make it difficult to approach the edge of the pond. Two parallel strings, set 15 cm (6 in) apart and 15 cm (6 in) from the edge of the pond, fixed one above the other with the upper at 35 cm (14 in) high, should do the trick.

Normally, a great spotted woodpecker would be a most welcome guest in anybody's garden. With the proliferation of nest boxes, however, they have learned to visit gardens to raid them for the young, chipping their way in when necessary. The metal plate referred to on page 59 is the only effective defence against this, and will deter squirrels, too, unless you use a nest box made of plastic or earthenware. Wooden nest boxes can also have their edges protected with metal strips.

MAMMALS

Squirrels have already been discussed in relation to feeders and nest boxes, and if the recommended deterrents don't work, trapping and releasing far away is the best answer. If a trap is used, for example in a loft that the squirrels have entered, it must be checked daily to ensure that the trapped animal doesn't starve to death. Rats may also be attracted to the garden by food put out for birds, and can be trapped in the same manner. Poison is not advised, especially if there are dogs or cats around, which may be deterrents in themselves anyway.

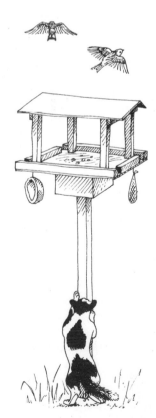

Domestic cats are probably the greatest predators of garden birds.

Cats are probably the greatest predators of garden birds. As with the squirrel problem, much can be done to protect birds at the feeder or nest box, but sometimes all fails. It is particularly galling if the offender is a neighbour's pet, while if you have a cat yourself you should think very carefully before attracting birds in to face the danger. The worst birders are female cats that spend all their time outside, supplementing their cat food with whatever else they can catch. A dog will, of course, frighten away a cat when it is out in the garden, but unless it regularly harasses cats it may not be particularly effective.

Weasels and long-tailed field mice are both expert climbers and may take a heavy toll on eggs and young, preying particularly on nest boxes. Suspending a nest box, with a cone on the suspension wire, should deter, and siting nest boxes in thorns is a natural remedy. If this fails, you may have to resort to trapping. An effective mouse deterrent is to press anti-mouse pellets (available from certain seed merchants) into the bark of the tree around the nest box.

In the garden, as in a wood, there is an order among the animals which depends upon some being the prey of others. Robins eat worms, song thrushes smash open snails on an anvil to eat them, and kestrels feed mainly on voles. Although life and death may seem more sharply defined within the limits of the garden, it is important to keep things in perspective, bearing in mind that the garden is, after all, only a smaller version of the greater natural world outside it.

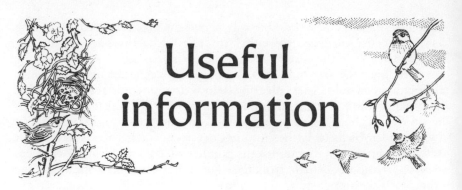

Useful information

SICK AND INJURED BIRDS

CAPTURE AND HANDLING
Once you are sure that a bird requires help it must be captured with a minimum of distress to the bird. Covering it first with a large box or blanket (to put it into the dark) will assist capture. Handling must be firm but gentle, with the wings held close to the body to prevent injury. Transfer the bird to a box placed in a warm, quiet place. Wear gloves to protect your hands from birds of prey, and keep your face away from owls, herons, gannets and other sharp-beaked birds. Wrap the wings of swans and geese to confine the birds. Wash your hands after handling. Keep injured birds away from pet birds.

TREATMENT
Small wounds can be cleaned with mild antiseptic and water and will heal quickly. More serious wounds need treatment by a vet. For shock, keep the bird in a dark box in a warm, quiet place for at least one hour. If the bird is ill enough to pick up, recovery is unlikely. NB The RSPB does not employ veterinary staff, and has no facilities for the care of sick birds.

HOUSING
Rabbit-hutch accommodation is ideal. Supply a perch if the bird is fit enough to use it. Cover the floor with thick newspaper and change daily. Place food and water where the bird can reach it easily. Raise the temperature to 21°C (70°F) if the bird is very ill; up to 30°C (86°F) for the smallest birds.

FOODS
Seed-eaters (finches, buntings, sparrows): proprietary seed-mix from pet-shop.

Insect-eaters (including robins, dunnocks, blackbirds, thrushes and tits): 'softbill' food from the petshop or scrambled egg and moist crushed cereal for a stop-gap; also strips of lean meat, but these and any food for a young bird need vitamin-mineral supplement.

Larger birds will take scraps, soaked puppy biscuit and tinned dog and cat food. Remove uneaten food.

ORPHAN BIRDS
See text regarding apparently abandoned baby birds. If it is essential to take the bird into your care, be prepared for a long, messy job. Regular feeding (once an hour) is essential during daylight; you must also remove faeces after each feed. Blunt forceps or tweezers, or a small paintbrush can be used to administer crushed, soaked biscuit with scrambled egg and thin strips of ox-heart or chopped-up earthworm, plus a vitamin supplement. Water in the food will suffice for a drink. Touch the beak to encourage

gaping. If this does not work, gently prise open the beak with thumb and forefinger while someone else gives the food. When tiny, make an artificial nest and keep the bird warm. An airing cupboard is ideal at night. When the bird is more active, transfer to the cage and leave food in to encourage self-feeding.

RELEASE

When fit or fledged the bird must be released as soon as possible. Take the cage to the place where the bird was found (or to a similar site if this is not possible) at the break of a fine day. Leave the bird for an hour or two before release. Release owls at dusk. You may need to keep feeding for a day or two, at regular times, as in captivity.

OTHER POINTS

Birds beyond recovery should be humanely destroyed.

If you encounter oiled birds you should contact the RSPCA; do not attempt to clean the bird yourself.

All birds of prey (except owls) are required by law to be kept by a registered keeper; contact the RSPCA or RSPB regional office. This same law applies to most Schedule 1 birds (see below).

(This information is summarized from the joint RSPB/RSPCA leaflet obtainable from the RSPB. Enclose SAE.)

BIRDS AND THE LAW

The following is summarized from the leaflet 'Information about birds and the law', available from the RSPB.

The Wildlife and Countryside Act 1981 supersedes the 1954 Protection of Birds Act. All birds, their nests and eggs are protected by law and it is an offence, with certain exceptions, to intentionally:

1 Kill, injure or take any wild bird;

2 Take, damage or destroy the nest of any wild bird whilst it is in use or being built;

3 Take or destroy the egg of any wild bird;

4 Have in one's possession or control any wild bird (dead or alive) or any part of a wild bird which has been taken in contravention of the Act or the Protection of Birds Act 1954;

5 Have in one's possession or control any egg or part of an egg which has been taken in contravention of the Act;

6 Have in one's possession or control any live bird of prey of any species in the world (except Old World vultures), unless it is registered and ringed in accordance with the Secretary of State's regulations;

7 Have in one's possession or control any bird of a species occurring on Schedule 4 of the Act unless registered (and in some cases ringed) in accordance with the Secretary of State's regulations;

8 Disturb any wild bird on Schedule 1 while it is nest building, or at a nest containing eggs or young, or disturb the dependent young of such a bird.

SALE OF LIVE WILD BIRDS AND THEIR EGGS

Unless appropriately licensed it is an offence to sell, offer for sale, possess or transport for sale or exchange:

1 Any live bird unless listed on Schedule 3, Part 1 and then only if aviary bred and close-ringed with an approved ring as defined by the Secretary of State's regulations;

2 The egg of any wild bird (whether or not taken in contravention of the Act).

It is illegal to attempt to commit any offence or have in one's possession anything capable of being used to commit an offence.

OTHER WILDLIFE AND THE LAW

Schedule 5 of the Wildlife and Countryside Act also protects the following: all bats (it is also an offence to disturb roosting bats or destroy any place which they are using for shelter); otter; common porpoise, and common and bottle-nosed dolphins; red squirrel; smooth snake; sand lizard; great crested newt; natterjack toad; burbot; fen-raft and ladybird spiders; wart-biter grasshopper; rainbow leaf beetle; field and mole crickets; chequered skipper, heath fritillary, Norfolk aeshna, large blue and swallowtail butterflies; barberry carpet, black-veined, Essex emerald, New Forest burnet and reddish buff moths; Carthusian, glutinous and sandbowl snails.

Additionally it is an offence to sell adders, common frogs, common lizards, palmate and smooth newts, slow worms, grass snakes and common toads; or their spawn (where appropriate).

It is also an offence to uproot any wild plant (except for some noxious weeds) unless you are an authorized person – the owner or occupier of the land, or someone with the permission of the owner or occupier. Additionally it is illegal to pick, uproot or destroy a small number of specially protected plants, all of which are extremely rare and endangered. It is legal to pick fungi (mushrooms and toadstools) and most seaweeds, however.

PESTICIDES AND THE GARDENER

Only use a pesticide if you can identify what is affecting your plants – pesticides may affect harmless species as well as the pests for which they are intended. Generally, keep chemicals out of reach of children and pets. Avoid contaminating any water – fishes are particularly susceptible to chemicals, even when diluted. Avoid spraying plants when they are in flower to reduce the risks to pollinating insects. Be careful not to let your spray drift with the wind, for it can seriously affect your herbaceous plants. Only spray problem weeds when absolutely necessary, and avoid contaminating neighbouring areas, as your 'weed' may be wild bird food! The following herbicides and insecticides are recommended as causing the least harm to other wildlife, but organic gardening is strongly recommended. Chemicals named are active ingredients of products sold under proprietary brand names.

If chemicals are to be used then the following are recommended. For clovers, daisies, dandelions, plantains, nettles, docks, coltsfoot, horsetail and bindweed: 2,4-D or mecoprop. For winter moths on fruit trees, aphids on fruit trees before blossoming, cutworms, onion fly, carrot fly, sawfly and cabbage fly, codling moth and caterpillars on vegetables: chlorpyrifos. For thrips, red spider mite, raspberry beetle and caterpillars: derris or malathion. Malathion may also be used against aphids on vegetables. For blackcurrant gall mite: lime sulphur. For wasps: carbaryl. There is now available a new organic pesticide derived from toxins existing in plants.

BIRDWATCHERS' CODE

1 The welfare of the birds must come first;
2 Habitat must be protected;
3 Keep disturbance to birds and their habitats to a minimum;
4 When you find a rare bird think carefully about whom you should tell;
5 Do not harass rare migrants;
6 Abide by the Bird Protection Acts at all times;
7 Respect the rights of landowners;
8 Respect the rights of other people in the countryside;
9 Make your records available to the local bird recorder for they may help to build up a picture of bird movements;
10 Behave abroad as you would when birdwatching at home.

USEFUL ADDRESSES

ORGANIZATIONS

British Butterfly Conservation Society, Tudor House, Quorn, Nr. Loughborough, Leicestershire LE12 8AD.

Botanical Society of the British Isles, c/o Dept. of Botany, British Museum (Natural History), Cromwell Road, London SW7 5BD.

Flora and Fauna Preservation Society, c/o Zoological Society of London, Regent's Park, London NW1 4RY.

Irish Wildlife Conservancy, Southview, Church Road, Greystones, Co. Wicklow.

Scottish Wildlife Trust, 25 Johnston Terrace, Edinburgh EH1 2NH.

The British Trust for Ornithology, Beech Grove, Station Road, Tring, Hertfordshire HP23 5NR.

The Henry Doubleday Research Association, 20 Convent Lane, Bocking, Braintree, Essex CN7 6RW. (The Association undertakes research into organic gardening and natural control of garden pests. Publishes occasional bulletins.)

The Royal Society for Nature Conservation, The Green, Nettleham, Lincoln LN2 2NR.

The Royal Society for the Prevention of Cruelty to Animals, The Causeway, Horsham, West Sussex RH12 1HG.

The Royal Society for the Protection of Birds, The Lodge, Sandy, Bedfordshire SG19 2DL.

The Woodland Trust, Westgate, Grantham, Lincolnshire NG3 6LL.

Young Ornithologist's Club – as RSPB.

FURTHER READING

BIRDWATCHING BOOKS
Birdwatcher's Britain by John Parslow (Pan).
Birdwatcher's Yearbook edited by John E. Pemberton (Buckingham Press).
RSPB Book of British Birds by Peter Holden, J.T.R. Sharrock and Hilary Burn (Macmillan).
The Birdlife of Britain by Peter Hayman and Philip Burton (Mitchell Beazley in association with RSPB).
The Mitchell Beazley Birdwatcher's Pocket Guide by Peter Hayman (Mitchell Beazley).
The Shell Guide to the Birds of Britain and Ireland by James Ferguson-Lees, Ian Willis and J.T.R. Sharrock (Michael Joseph).
What's That Bird? by Michael Everett and Peter Hayman (RSPB).

GARDENING BOOKS
The Complete Book of Self-sufficiency by John Seymour (Corgi).
The Tree and Shrub Expert by Dr D.G. Hessayon (Pan Britannica Industries Ltd).

GENERAL BOOKS
The Family Naturalist by Michael Chinery (MacDonald and Jane's).

REFERENCE SOURCES ACKNOWLEDGED BY THE AUTHOR IN THE PREPARATION OF THIS BOOK
A Field Guide to the Birds of Britain and Europe by Roger Peterson, Guy Mountfort and P.A.D. Hollom (Collins).
Bird Life by Dr Christopher Perrins (Elsevier/Phaidon).
Birds of the World (IPC partwork edited by John Gooders).
Gardening with Wildlife edited by Nicholas Hammond (RSPB). The RSPB also produces several other useful leaflets on gardening and wildlife.
The Back Garden Wildlife Sanctuary Book by Ron Wilson (Astragal Books).
The Birds of the British Isles and their eggs by T.A. Coward (Warne).
The Complete Guide to British Wildlife by R.S. Fitter (Collins).
The Concise Flora in Colour by W. Keble-Martin (Ebury Press and Michael Joseph).
The Garden Bird Book edited by David Glue (Macmillan).
The Handbook of British Birds edited by H.F. Witherby (Witherby).
The Natural History of the Garden by Michael Chinery (Collins).
The Shell Bird Book by James Fisher (Ebury Press and Michael Joseph).
The Bird Table Book by Tony Soper (David and Charles).

Index